| | |
|---|---|
| **Parent Letter** | iv |
| **Inside** Summer Bridge Activities™ for Young Christians | v |
| **10 Helpful Hints on How to Maximize Your Child's Character** | vi |
| **1 Corinthians Christian Character Checklist** | vii |
| **Encourage Your Child to Read the Bible** | viii |
| **Reading Book List** | ix |

**1st Section** .................................................................................................................1
    Motivational Calendar .......................................................................................1
    Day 1 through Day 15—Daily Activities in Math, Reading,
                  Writing, and Language Arts ........................................................3
    Words to Sound, Read, and Spell ...................................................................33

**2nd Section** ..............................................................................................................35
    Motivational Calendar .....................................................................................35
    Day 1 through Day 20—Daily Activities in Math, Reading,
                  Writing, and Language Arts ......................................................37
    Words to Sound, Read, and Spell ...................................................................77

**3rd Section** ..............................................................................................................79
    Motivational Calendar .....................................................................................79
    Day 1 through Day 15—Daily Activities in Math, Reading,
                  Writing, and Language Arts ......................................................81
    Words to Sound, Read, and Spell .................................................................111

**Answer Pages** ........................................................................................................113

**SBAYC Vacation Bible Camp** ..............................................................................127

**Flashcards: Addition and Subtraction 0–10, and**
                Alphabet Sound Cards ...............................................................................149

**Certificate of Completion** ..........................................................................Last Page

www.summerbrains.com      © Summer Bridge Activities™ 1–2

# Dear Parents,

**T**hank you for choosing *Summer Bridge Activities™ for Young Christians* to help reinforce you children's classroom skills while away from school. This year, we are proud to offer you this unique addition, which contains ways to help your children develop their minds and further their Christian walk this summer. This book is full of skill-building activities to reinforce the valuable academics that your children need, coupled with exercises and ideas to foster their Christian growth.

**F**amily is the foundation of life. That is why it is imperative that you work with your children to help them be the best they can be—the best Christians, the best students, the best citizens. As parents, you must instill core values that will stay with your children throughout their lives. We created this book to assist you, as a parent, as you foster your child's academic and spiritual development. Inside, you will find helpful introductory material with valuable resources and ideas for building your child's Christian character, including a book list containing classic children's literature along with Christian resources to further strengthen your child's mind and spirit. This section is followed by ten weeks of daily, age-appropriate academic activities. The book wraps up with a bonus Bible Camp Section. The activities in the bonus section are intended to be completed alongside daily academic skill reinforcement.

**T**his book is different from other skill-building books, for while its obvious goal is to build and maintain academic skills over the summer, it also encourages your children to enhance their spiritual skills as well. At the beginning of each day, you and your children are encouraged to complete a short daily devotional to help get them focused not only on the task before them but also to start the entire day in the right frame of mind—on God. The daily devotionals are made up of Bible verses and quotes that foster a positive character and a Christian attitude.

**W**e hope that you and your children get the most out of *Summer Bridge Activities™ for Young Christians*. May God bless you as you strive to help your children build a strong bridge to success in the classroom and in life!

Sincerely,

Michele D. Van Leeuwen      Sabena Maiden

# Summer Bridge Activities™ for Young Christians

## First Grade to Second Grade

SBA was created by
**Michele D. Van Leeuwen**

written by
**Julia Ann Hobbs
Carla Dawn Fisher
Sabena Maiden**

exercise illustrations by
**Amanda Sorensen**

## This Book Contains...

- Fun, skill-based activities in **reading, writing, arithmetic,** and **language arts** to keep your child busy, happy, and learning! *Summer Bridge Activities™ for Young Christians* is divided into three sections for review and preview with pages numbered by day. Children complete their work quickly with the easy-to-use format, leaving lots of time for play!

- A summer **Reading List** based on the Accelerated Reader Program and classic Christian titles.

- A **Motivational Calendar** to encourage summer learning and reward your child's efforts. **"Discover Something New"** lists of creative things to do are found on the back of each *Summer Bridge Activities™ for Young Christians* Motivational Calendar for when your child says the inevitable: "What can I do? I'm bored."

- Comprehensive **Word Lists**, which contain words to sound, read, and spell, challenge children and encourage them to build their vocabulary. *Summer Bridge Activities™ for Young Christians* 1–2 also contains **Addition and Subtraction Flashcards, 0–10** and **Alphabet Sound Flashcards** to reinforce these skills.

- **Tear-out answer pages** to help correct your child's work.

- An official **Certificate of Completion** to be awarded for successfully completing the workbook.

Mr. Fredrickson

Here are some groups who think our books are great!

Ms. Hansen

Hey Kids and Parents!
Log online to
www.summerbrains.com for
more eye-boggling, mind-bending,
brain-twisting summer fun...
It's where summerbrains
like you hang out!
www.summerbrains.com

# Summer Bridge Activities™ for Young Christians
## 1st to 2nd Grade

All rights reserved.
© 2005 Carson-Dellosa Publishing Company, Inc.
Greensboro, North Carolina 27425

The purchase of this material entitles the buyer to reproduce worksheets and activities for classroom use only—not for commercial resale. Reproduction of these materials for an entire school or district is prohibited. No part of this book may be reproduced (except as noted above), stored in a retrieval system, or transmitted in any form or by any means (mechanically, electronically, recording, etc.) without the prior written consent of Carson-Dellosa Publishing Co., Inc.

Scripture taken from the HOLY BIBLE, NEW INTERNATIONAL VERSION®.
Copyright © 1973, 1978, 1984, International Bible Society. Used by permission of Zondervan Bible Publishers.
All rights reserved.

---

### RBP thanks those involved in the creation of this book:
Kathleen Bratcher, Andy Carlson, Suzie Ellison, Russ Flint, Robyn Funk,
Randy Harward, Jerold Johnson, Zack Johnson, Kristina Kugler, Carol Layton,
Dante J. Orazzi, Paul Rawlins, Debra Reed, Amanda Sorensen, George Starks,
Michele D. Van Leeuwen, Scott G. Van Leeuwen, Jennifer Willes

---

Please visit our website at
www.summerbridgeactivities.com
for supplements, additions, and corrections to this book.

First Edition 2005

ISBN: 1-594412-82-0

PRINTED IN THE UNITED STATES OF AMERICA
10 9 8 7 6 5 4 3 2 1

## Ms. Hansen TAKES YOU INSIDE Summer Bridge Activities™ for Young Christians

The exercises that are found in *Summer Bridge Activities™ for Young Christians* (SBAYC) are easy to understand and are presented in a way that allows your child to review familiar skills and then be progressively challenged on more difficult subjects. In addition to academic exercises, SBAYC contains many other activities to challenge and reinforce your children's knowledge of the Bible and further develop their Christian walk with God.

### Sections of SBAYC

 There are three sections in SBAYC; the first and second review, the third previews.

 Each section begins with an SBAYC Motivational Calendar.

 Each day your child will complete an activity in reading, writing, arithmetic, and language skills. The activities progressively become more challenging.

 Each page is numbered by day. Have your child start the day by reading the daily devotional.

 Your child will need a pencil, ruler, eraser, and crayons to complete the activities.

### Books Children Love to Read

 SBAYC contains a Reading Book List with a variety of titles, including many that are found in the Accelerated Reader Program. In addition, you will find many quality books by Christian authors. Christian resources are noted with a †.

 We recommend that parents read to their pre-kindergarten through 1st grade children 5 to 10 minutes each day and then ask questions about the story to reinforce comprehension. For higher grade levels, we recommend the following daily reading times: grades 1–2, 10 to 20 minutes; grades 2–3, 20 to 30 minutes; grades 3–4, 30 to 45 minutes; grades 4–5 and 5–6, 45 to 60 minutes.

 It is important that the parent and child decide an amount of reading time and write it on the SBAYC Motivational Calendar.

### SBAYC Motivational Calendars

- Calendars are located at the beginning of each section.
- We suggest that the parent and child sign the SBAYC Motivational Calendar before the child begins each section.
- When your child completes one day of SBAYC, he/she may color or initial the star.
- Refer to the recommended reading times. When your child completes the agreed reading time each day, he/she may color or initial the book.
- The parent may also initial the SBAYC Motivational Calendar once the activities have been completed.
- We recommend completing the daily devotional and marking it on the calendar before doing the academic exercises so your child begins the day's activities focused and ready.

www.summerbrains.com © Summer Bridge Activities™ 1–2

# 10 Helpful Hints on How to Maximize your child's character.

 1. Read the Bible with your children every day. Point out specific examples of how God recognizes those who show good character.

 2. Be a good example to your children. Exhibit the behaviors and standards that you want to see them use. Sometimes children can learn more from what you do than what you say.

 3. With your children, define what good character means to your family. Identify specific traits, such as respect and honesty, that you want your family to strive for.

 4. Make a Family Character Chart. When a family member displays good character, indicate it on the chart with a sticker or check mark. Build in a special family incentive, such as a special family dinner or trip, for when a family goal has been reached.

 5. Recognize when someone in the family has displayed good Christian character. Mention it in front of the entire family at dinner or some other time when the family is together. Acknowledging positive examples presents a clear message that good character is important in your family (and recognizing good character may have a contagious effect).

 6. Post your family's values for all to see. This may be done by posting a list of the house rules and goals on the refrigerator, or it may be a mission statement cross-stitched and hung in a frame. Make it simple enough so that even your youngest child will understand your family's values.

 7. Make fun character craft projects and activities to serve as friendly reminders, particularly when certain family values are not being remembered. These can be fun, simple ideas, such as a mobile that lists each Christian character trait that your family has agreed upon or cookies with kind words to each other written in icing.

 8. Provide your children with positive role models through quality resources. There are many books, magazines, youth organizations, music concerts, websites, videos, and DVDs that promote good values and character. Make them available to your children.

 9. Encourage your children to be charitable. There are many ways that your family can get involved with helping others. Whether you volunteer regularly at a soup kitchen or have a monthly family collection of used clothes, toys, and other household items to give to a local charity, show your children how much helping others enriches everyone's lives. This will also provide numerous "hands-on" opportunities for strengthening character.

 10. Talk to your children and listen to them as they share their thoughts, ideas, and opinions. An important part of establishing your family's good values begins with your children feeling valued themselves.

# "Love Never Fails" (1 Corinthians 13:4–8)

The Bible speaks a great deal about God's love for us. **1 John 4:8** even tells us that "God is love." And because God loves each of us so much, we, too, should share that incredible gift with others. The way to show Christian character is to display love in our daily actions. God provides us the ultimate example of Christian character that each person should strive for. **Exodus 34:6–7** refers to God as "The LORD, the LORD, the compassionate and gracious God, slow to anger, abounding in love and faithfulness, maintaining love to thousands, and forgiving wickedness, rebellion and sin."

Use this checklist with your family as a daily reminder of how they can exemplify Christian character through loving actions.

## Today I can show my best Christian character by...

- being patient with others, even when it is difficult.
  *Love is patient,*

- showing kindness to others.
  *love is kind.*

- being content with the things that I have.
  *It does not envy,*

- using kind, encouraging words when I speak.
  *it does not boast,*

- being respectful and not showing off.
  *it is not proud.*

- showing a positive attitude.
  *It is not rude,*

- looking to see how I can help others, not just myself.
  *it is not selfseeking,*

- being calm and not using anger in a hurtful way.
  *it is not easily angered,*

- forgiving others and not holding grudges.
  *it keeps no record of wrongs.*

- doing activities that please the Lord.
  *Love does not delight in evil but rejoices with the truth.*

*God is love.*

 Make fun games based on your family's favorite board games or game shows. Prepare questions and answers based on biblical facts, and use the rules from the original game. This is a great activity for family game night.

 Help your children learn the books of the Bible in order using a fun, made-up tune or familiar song.

 Conduct family "Sword Drills." Call out a specific chapter and verse reference, and see who can find it first to read to the family. This is a great way for your children to learn the order of the books in the Bible.

 Familiarize your children with Scripture by making a Bible treasure hunt. Pose questions to your children that will require them to search through the scriptures for the answers.

 Buy your child a study Bible specific to his or her age and reading level.

 Regularly tell your children stories from Scripture. No child is too young to listen to a bedtime story or hear an interesting true tale while in the car. Share a Bible story with your children either from memory or use a good Bible storybook. (There are many wonderful Christian resources available in print and on the Web.)

 Read the Bible with your children. Make it a daily habit to share a special verse at breakfast or before going to bed.

 Read your Bible. Let your children see you enjoying the Word of God daily. Also, share specific things from your reading that your children can benefit from and understand.

# Reading Book List

**Ackerman, Karen**
  Song and Dance Man
**Allard, Harry**
  Miss Nelson Is Missing!
**Andersen, Hans Christian**
**(retold by Anne Rockwell)**
  The Emperor's New Clothes
**Arnold, Tedd**
  No Jumping on the Bed
**Bishop, Jennie**
  Jesus Must Really Be Special †
**Bonsall, Crosby**
  And I Mean It, Stanley
  Mine's the Best
**Brown, Marcia**
  Stone Soup, an Old Tale
**Cerf, Bennett**
  Bennett Cerf's Book of Laughs
  Bennett Cerf's Book of Riddles
**Cohen, Barbara**
  Molly's Pilgrim
**Cosgrove, Stephen**
  Leo the Lop—I, II, III
  Hucklebug
  Snaffles
**Dicks, Terrance**
  Adventures of Goliath Series
**Duvoisin, Roger**
  Petunia
**Eastman, P. D.**
  Are You My Mother?
**Freeman, Don**
  Corduroy

**Gordon, Sharon**
  Play Ball, Kate!
**Gregorich, Barbara**
  Beep, Beep
**Grimm, Jacob and Wilhelm**
**(The Brothers Grimm)**
  The Frog Prince
**Hall, Donald**
  Ox-Cart Man
**Hall, Kirsten**
  Bunny, Bunny
**Hutchins, Pat**
  Don't Forget the Bacon!
  Good Night, Owl!
  Rosie's Walk
**Isadora, Rachel**
  My Ballet Class
**Kellogg, Steven**
  Paul Bunyan, a Tall Tale
**Leaf, Munro**
  The Story of Ferdinand
  Wee Gillis
**LeSieg, Theo**
  The Eye Book
**Lobel, Arnold**
  Frog and Toad series
**Lopshire, Robert**
  Put Me in the Zoo
**Loth, Paul J.**
  My First Study Bible †
**MacArthur, John**
  A Faith to Grow On †
**McCloskey, Robert**
  Make Way for Ducklings

**McDonald, Mindy**
  My Bible Storybook †
**Minarik, Else Holmelund**
  Little Bear
**Moore, Beth**
  A Parable about the King †
**Peet, Bill**
  The Ant and the Elephant
  Buford, the Little Bighorn
  The Caboose Who Got Loose
**Peretti, Frank**
  Wild & Wacky Totally True Bible Stories †
**Perkins, Al**
  The Nose Book
**Sendak, Maurice**
  Higglety Pigglety Pop!
**Dr. Seuss**
  The Cat in the Hat
  Green Eggs and Ham
  The Foot Book
**Sharmat, Marjorie Weinman**
  Nate the Great and the Musical Note
**Shaw, Nancy**
  Sheep in Jeep
**Slobodkina, Esphyr**
  Caps for Sale
**Smouse, Phil**
  Jesus Wants All of Me †
**Steig, William**
  Roland the Minstrel Pig
**Tada, Joni Eareckson**
  You've Got a Friend †

**Thomas, Joan Gale**
  If Jesus Came to My House †
**Trent, John**
  The Two Trails †
**Viorst, Judith**
  Alexander and the Terrible, Horrible, No Good, Very Bad Day
**Waber, Bernard**
  Ira Sleeps Over
**Ward, Lynd**
  The Biggest Bear
**Wiseman, Bernard**
  Morris and Boris at the Circus
**Yolen, Jane**
  Picnic with Piggins
**Ziefert, Harriet**
  Harry Gets Ready for School
**Zobel-Nolan, Allia and Tommy Nelson**
  Who Does God Love? †

† Indicates Christian Resource

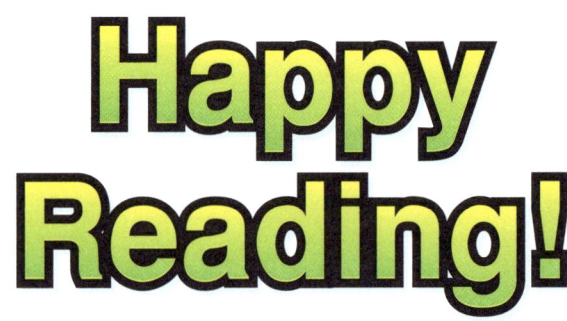

Summer Bridge Activities™ for Young Christians

# Motivational Calendar!

Month _____

My parents and I decided that if I complete 15 days of *Summer Bridge Activities™ for Young Christians* and read _____ minutes a day, my incentive/reward will be:

_____

Child's Signature _____ Parent's Signature _____

Day 1   ☆ 🕊 📖 ____         Day 9   ☆ 🕊 📖 ____
Day 2   ☆ 🕊 📖 ____         Day 10  ☆ 🕊 📖 ____
Day 3   ☆ 🕊 📖 ____         Day 11  ☆ 🕊 📖 ____
Day 4   ☆ 🕊 📖 ____         Day 12  ☆ 🕊 📖 ____
Day 5   ☆ 🕊 📖 ____         Day 13  ☆ 🕊 📖 ____
Day 6   ☆ 🕊 📖 ____         Day 14  ☆ 🕊 📖 ____
Day 7   ☆ 🕊 📖 ____         Day 15  ☆ 🕊 📖 ____
Day 8   ☆ 🕊 📖 ____

**Child:** Color the ☆ for daily activities completed.
Color the 🕊 for daily devotionals completed.
Color the 📖 for daily reading completed.
**Parent:** Initial the ____ when your child is complete.

**Fun Activity Ideas to Go Along with the First Section!**

1. Set goals for your vacation time and post them on the refrigerator. Plan fun rewards.

2. Visit your local library. Obtain a library card and check out a book.

3. Plant a garden.

4. Make designs on the sidewalk with water.

5. Go on a nature walk. Collect ten assorted bugs and leaves and identify them.

6. Plan a reading picnic in the backyard park, or canyon.

7. Do some stargazing tonight. Find the Big Dipper.

8. Have a neighborhood waterfight.

9. Take a bus downtown with an adult and see a matinee movie.

10. Write a letter to a relative.

11. Go on a hike with a friend.

12. Surprise an elderly neighbor by weeding his or her garden.

13. Have a neighborhood baseball game.

14. Make up a play using old clothes as costumes.

15. Watch the sunset with your family.

**Write to 100.**

**John Fisher:** David wasn't thinking of being king when he was tending sheep; he was just doing what God sat before him.

# Day 1

| 1 | 2 |  |  | 5 |  |  |  |  | 10 |
|---|---|---|---|---|---|---|---|---|---|
|  |  |  | 14 |  |  |  |  | 19 |  |
|  |  | 23 |  |  |  | 27 |  |  |  |
| 31 |  |  |  | 35 |  |  |  |  |  |
|  | 42 |  |  |  |  |  | 48 |  |  |
|  |  |  |  |  | 56 |  |  |  | 60 |
|  |  |  | 64 |  |  |  |  | 69 |  |
|  |  | 73 |  |  |  | 76 |  |  |  |
| 81 |  |  |  |  |  |  |  |  | 90 |
|  |  |  |  |  | 96 |  |  |  |  |

Circle the first letter underneath each picture if the picture begins with that sound. Circle the second letter if it ends with that sound. Color the pictures.

EXAMPLE:

(b)  b      k  k      n  n      l  l      p  p      t  t

r  r      s  s      j  j      h  h      m  m      c  c

www.summerbrains.com
© Summer Bridge Activities™ 1–2

# Day 1

**Write the capital letters of the alphabet.**

EXAMPLE:

A B _____

**Circle and write the correct word.**

EXAMPLE:

| | | | | | |
|---|---|---|---|---|---|
| 1. | We will go in the ____van____. | (van) | can | ran |
| 2. | I can help the _____. | mat | man | tan |
| 3. | I am a good_____. | book | moon | cook |
| 4. | He is in his _____. | red | bed | fan |
| 5. | Can you get a _____? | the | it | book |
| 6. | I am a _____man. | sad | glass | sled |
| 7. | Find the big_____. | tug | pig | pink |
| 8. | Where is the _____? | hid | run | flag |
| 9. | I can run and _____. | jump | cup | went |
| 10. | I will take a hot _____. | moth | bath | tooth |

**Add or subtract.**

**Deuteronomy 6:5**
Love the LORD your God with all your heart and with all your soul and with all your strength.

**Day 2**

| 3 | 4 | 5 | 2 | 0 | 8 | 1 | 7 |
|---|---|---|---|---|---|---|---|
| +2 | +3 | +0 | +1 | +1 | +1 | +5 | +2 |

| 4 | 9 | 7 | 6 | 5 | 3 | 0 | 8 |
|---|---|---|---|---|---|---|---|
| -2 | -3 | -7 | -4 | -1 | -2 | -0 | -5 |

| 9 | 0 | 3 | 8 | 4 | 7 | 5 | 5 |
|---|---|---|---|---|---|---|---|
| -4 | +6 | +5 | +2 | -3 | -5 | +5 | -3 |

**Circle the first letter in the box below each picture if the picture begins with that sound. Circle the second letter if the picture ends with that sound. Color the pictures.**

EXAMPLE:

| (f) f |  g g |  q q |  d d |  w w |  y y |
|---|---|---|---|---|---|

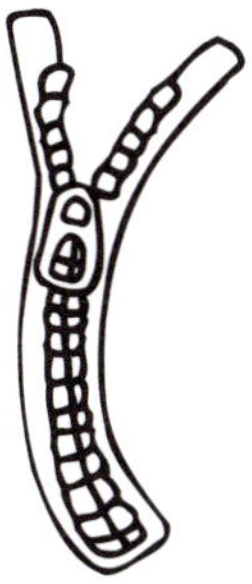

| z z |  p p |  f f | v v |  x x |  t t |
|---|---|---|---|---|---|

www.summerbrains.com

# Day 2

**Write the lowercase letters of the alphabet.**

EXAMPLE:
a b

**Practice reading these sentences. Draw a picture of your two favorite sentences.**

1. The dog is stuck in the mud.
2. The cat will sit on Ann's lap.
3. The boy has a pet frog.
4. The man sat on his hat.
5. The hat is flat and smashed.
6. The rat ran on Sam's bed.
7. Sam is mad at the bad rat.
8. Fred met a girl with a wig.
9. The little bug bit the duck.
10. Fran had a pretty red dress.

**Write the correct time on the small clocks. Draw hands on the big clocks.**

**1 Samuel 16:7**
"Man looks at the outward appearance, but the LORD looks at the heart."

**Day 3**

9:00      ___:___    7:00

___:___    3:00    ___:___

**Write the long vowel sound next to each picture. Color the picture.**

**Day**

Match the sentence with the correct picture. Write the sentence number in the box.

1. "Thank you for cleaning my yard!"
2. The ice cream truck is coming.
3. Rob buys two ice cream cones.
4. Rob and Tanner lick their ice cream.

Draw and color pictures to go with these words.

| bug | log | bed | bib |
|---|---|---|---|
| box | sit | rug | map |

**Complete the counting pattern.**

1  2  ___  ___  5  6  7  ___  ___  10  ___  ___
13  14  ___  16  ___  ___  19  ___  21  ___  ___  24  ___

31  ___  ___  34  ___  36  ___  ___  ___  40  41  ___  ___
44  ___  ___  47  ___  ___  50  ___  ___  53  ___  ___  ___

___  ___  77  78  ___  ___  ___  82  ___  84  ___  ___  87
88  ___  ___  ___  92  ___  ___  ___  96  ___  ___  ___  100

**Samuel Taylor Coleridge:** Our own heart, and not other men's opinions, forms our true honor.

**Day 4**

---

**Long and Short Vowels. Circle the correct word and color the picture.**

EXAMPLE:

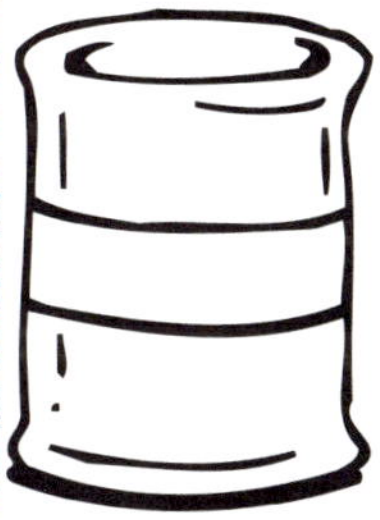

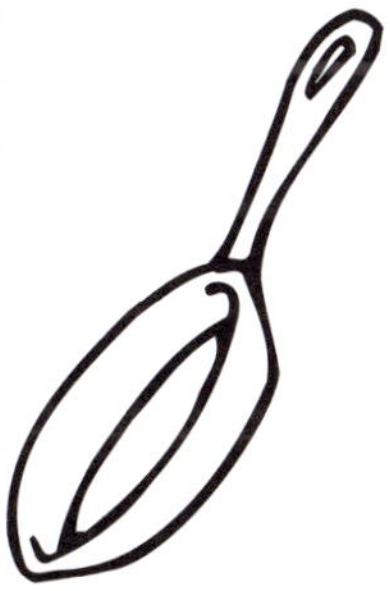

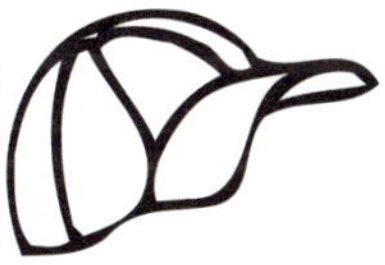

(can) cane | can cane | pin pine | pin pine | pane pan | cap cape

cub cube | cub cube | bite bit | past paste | rod rode | not note

**Day**

Practice writing your first and last name.

---

**End each sentence with the correct punctuation mark: (.), (!), or (?).**

**EXAMPLE:** Is your pet fat__?__

Do you like gum____

Jan can blow bubbles____

Can you jump a rope____

The woman was mad____

Are bears fuzzy____

Babies cry a lot____

Are clouds white____

Where is your Bible____

Did he drop the box____

Count the money and write in the amount.

**Psalm 23:1**
The LORD is my shepherd, I shall not be in want.

**Day 5**

 penny 1¢

 _____ ¢

 nickel 5¢

 _____ ¢

 dime 10¢

 _____ ¢

 _____ ¢

 quarter 25¢

 _____ ¢

Color the short vowel pictures blue and the long vowel pictures green.

 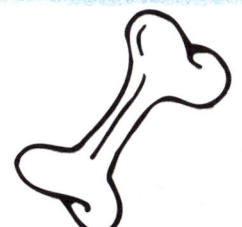  

www.summerbrains.com © Summer Bridge Activities™ 1–2

**Day** Circle words that rhyme with the first word.

EXAMPLE:

| 1. **cat** | (hat) | ham | (fat) | pig | (bat) | (rat) | (sat) |
|---|---|---|---|---|---|---|---|
| 2. **bag** | rag | tag | dog | lag | nag | big | sag |
| 3. **he** | she | me | we | go | see | be | tree |
| 4. **cake** | rake | late | lake | make | bake | stake | said |
| 5. **bank** | sank | drank | pink | sunk | tank | prank | rack |
| 6. **sing** | ring | song | thing | wing | bring | sting | big |
| 7. **run** | fun | gum | gun | sun | bun | spun | tin |
| 8. **coat** | moon | boat | goat | joke | shout | float | moat |
| 9. **look** | took | shoot | book | cook | rock | boost | hook |
| 10. **seat** | neat | wheat | treat | sleep | beat | sled | leap |

**Follow these directions and color your picture.**

1. Draw a tree.
2. Put a bird in your tree.
3. Draw a flower.
4. Draw a boy and his dog.
5. Draw a girl on a rock.
6. Give your picture a title.

**Count tens and ones.**

EXAMPLE:

 24   _____   _____

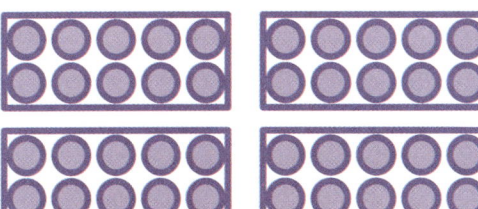

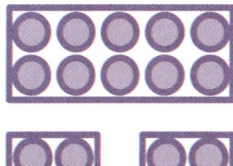 

 _____  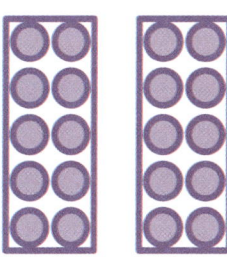 _____

 _____   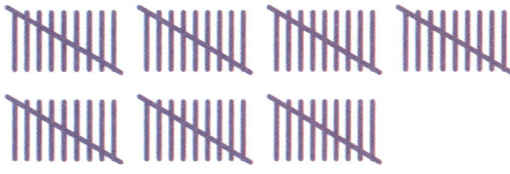 _____

---

**Write the short vowel below the picture.**

EXAMPLE:

      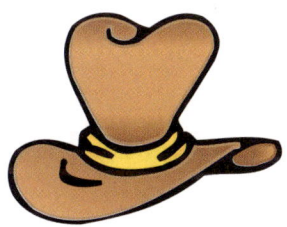   

o    ___    ___    ___

___   ___   ___   ___

**Day 6**

Psalm 25:4
Show me your ways, O LORD, teach me your paths.

**Day** Draw a line between the opposites.

EXAMPLE:

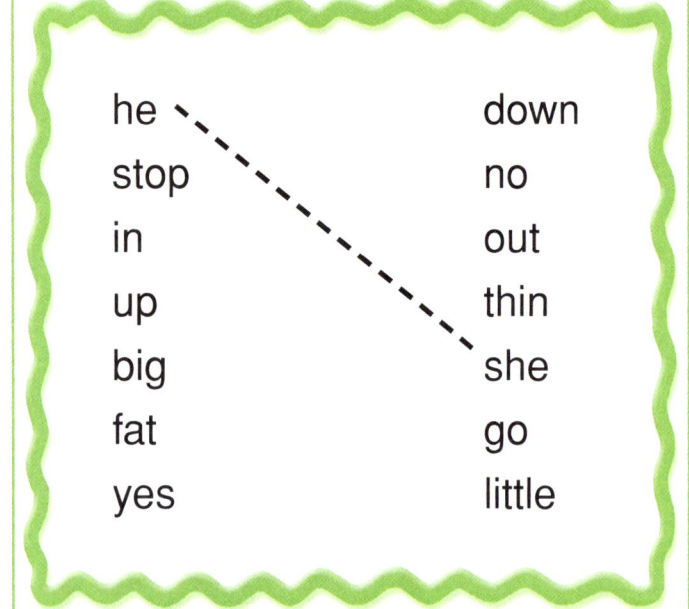

| he | down |
| stop | no |
| in | out |
| up | thin |
| big | she |
| fat | go |
| yes | little |

| soft | clean |
| hot | slow |
| fast | cold |
| left | hard |
| off | bottom |
| dirty | right |
| top | on |

Circle <u>yes</u> or <u>no</u>. Draw a picture of your favorite sentence.

1. Can a car jump?          yes     (no)
2. Can a rug be wet?        yes     no
3. Can men skip?            yes     no
4. Is a kitten a baby cat?  yes     no
5. Do fish have fins?       yes     no
6. Can feet hop and run?    yes     no
7. Do rocks need sleep?     yes     no
8. Can hats fly?            yes     no
9. Do cows give milk?       yes     no
10. Can a leg be sore?      yes     no
11. Can a baby cry?         yes     no
12. Can a boy sing?         yes     no
13. Can a bear swim?        yes     no
14. Can a cow eat a lot?    yes     no

**Read and answer these math problems.**

**Psalm 27:1**
The LORD is my light and my salvation—whom shall I fear?

**Day 7**

1. Grayson has two green cars and eight red cars in his train. How many cars does Grayson have in all?

_____ green cars   _____ red cars   _____ cars in train

2. There were five birds in one nest. Then two birds flew away. How many birds were left in the nest?

_____ − _____ = _____

3. Matt learned nine Bible verses on Monday. He forgot two of them by Friday. How many verses did he remember?

9 − 2 = _____

**For each set of words, write the contraction in the word blank.**

EXAMPLE:

1. it is     it's
2. you will  _____
3. I am      _____
4. we will   _____
5. they have _____
6. he will   _____

we'll   ~~it's~~   you'll   I'm   he'll   they've

**Day 7** Draw a picture the color of the word.

| blue | black | green |
| --- | --- | --- |
| yellow | purple | red |

**Circle the right word.**

1. boy
   bone
   can

2. bunny
   egg
   eye

3. sun
   sand
   snake

4. fish
   frog
   fan

5. yellow
   cow
   cat

6. book
   baby
   boat

7. six
   sat
   one

8. wish
   fish
   shop

9. rabbit
   mice
   dog

Count the money and write in the amount.

**Eleanor Roosevelt:** People grow through experience if they meet life honestly and courageously. This is how character is built.

# Day 8

EXAMPLE:

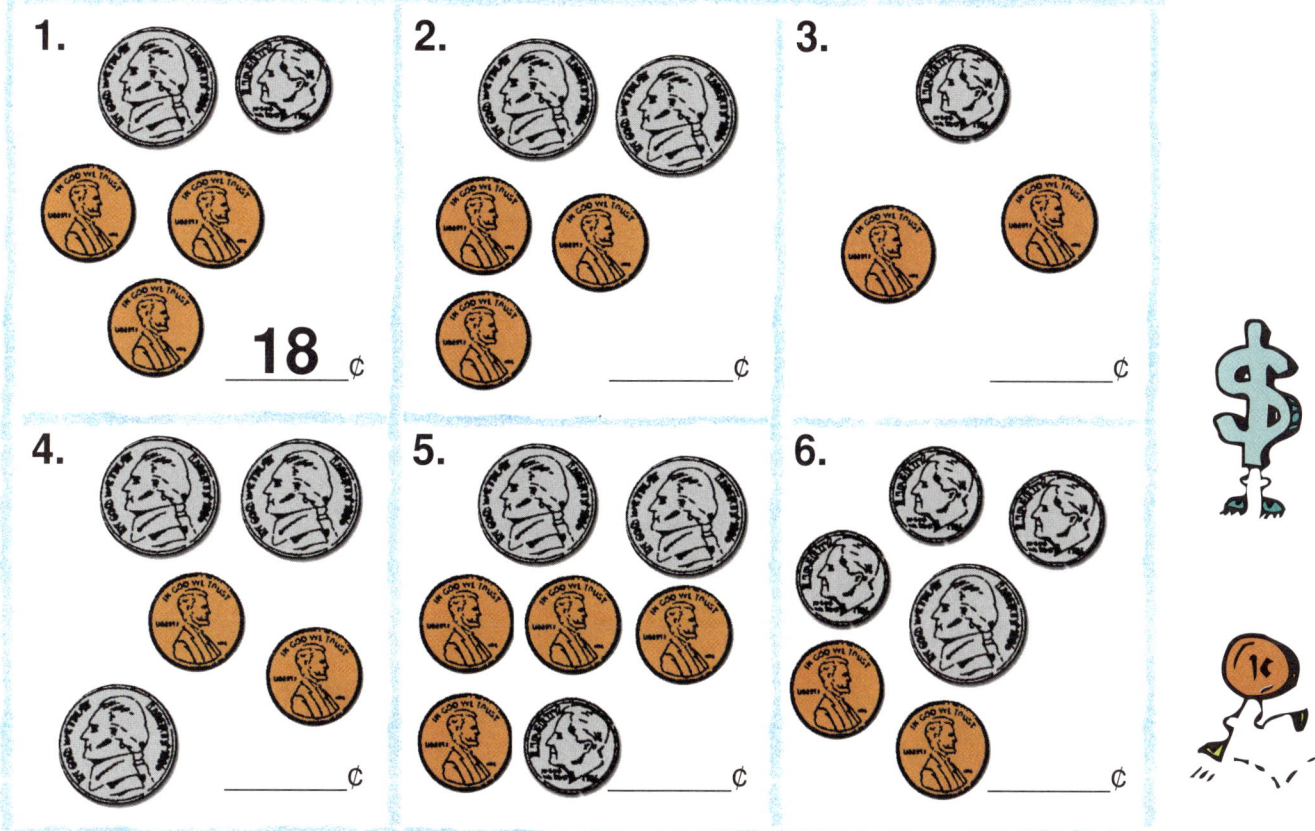

Write and finish this sentence in three different ways.
"I do what is right because…"

1. _____

2. _____

3. _____

**Day** In each sentence, draw a circle around the two words that rhyme. Color the picture.

1. The fish is in a dish.

2. The man in the boat is wearing a coat.

3. There is a bug in my mug.

4. The bee is in the tree.

**Put the words in alphabetical order.**

apple    1. _____
cat    2. _____
book    3. _____

girl    1. _____
ice    2. _____
hat    3. _____

hot    1. _____
sit    2. _____
cry    3. _____

dog    1. _____
fish    2. _____
elephant    3. _____

lamp    1. _____
king    2. _____
map    3. _____

well    1. _____
sleep    2. _____
dark    3. _____

**Match the price of each toy with the correct amount of money.**

**Psalm 68:19**
Praise be to the Lord, to God our Savior, who daily bears our burdens.

# Day 9

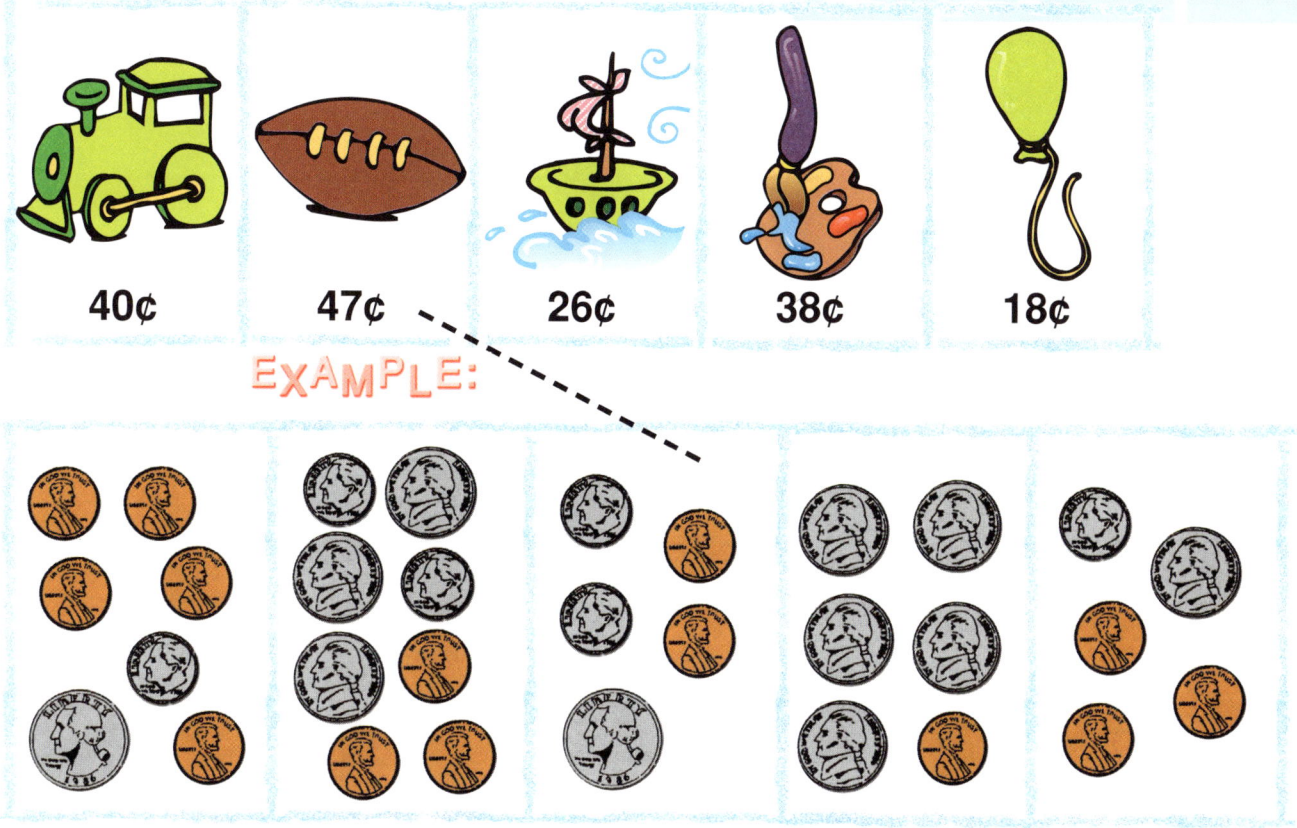

**Find and circle the words.**

EXAMPLE:

| I | F | L | Y | P | B | M | Y | W | C |
|---|---|---|---|---|---|---|---|---|---|
| D | C | C | M | I | D | T | A | I | L |
| E | F | E | H | E | I | I | G | L | I |
| H | I | G | H | G | M | E | U | D | M |
| N | I | G | H | T | E | I | Y | A | B |

~~ice~~   wild    my     fly
pie       high    guy    dime
night     climb   tie    tail

# Day 9

Write the color words that fit in the boxes.

yellow  orange  blue  black  purple
green  brown  red  gray  pink  white

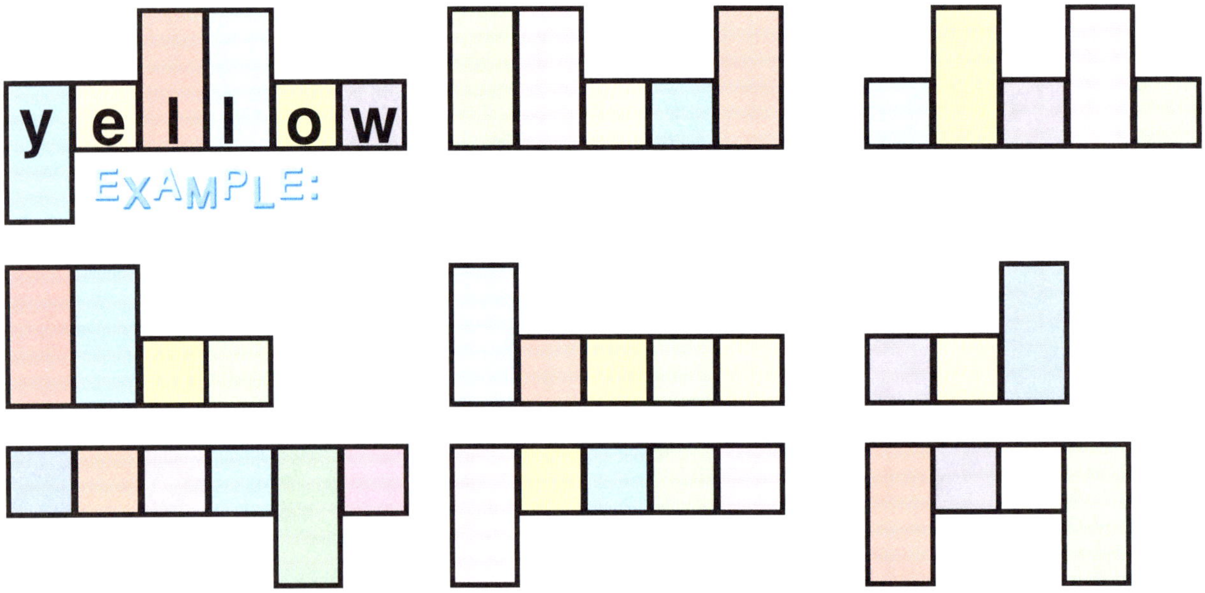

y e l l o w

EXAMPLE:

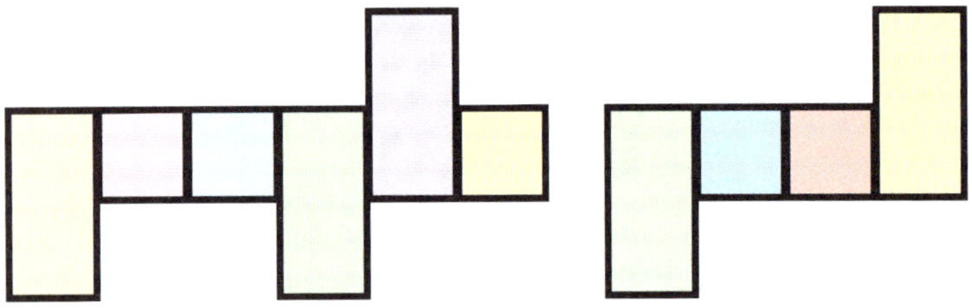

What is your favorite color?

_____

Put a (.) or a (?) at the end of each sentence. Draw a picture of your favorite sentence.

1. The dog ran down the road____
2. Do you like to play football____
3. Can a cat jump over a ditch____
4. We are going to church today____
5. What time do you go to bed____
6. Is green the color of a frog____
7. The farmer has ten horses____
8. Ann has a new blue dress____
9. We will walk to the store____
10. Will your mom go swimming with us____

Add or subtract.

**Psalm 95:1**
Come, let us sing for joy to the LORD; let us shout aloud to the Rock of our salvation.

**Day 10**

5 + 6 = _____     6 + 4 = _____     3 + 8 = _____

7 + 3 = _____     9 − 5 = _____     6 − 4 = _____

10 + 1 = _____    8 − 3 = _____     2 + 9 = _____

8 − 2 = _____     10 − 4 = _____    9 − 3 = _____

10 − 5 = _____    8 + 2 = _____     9 + 3 = _____

6 + 5 = _____     7 + 4 = _____     8 + 0 = _____

---

Match each sentence with the correct job title.

EXAMPLE:

I like to fish. -------- farmer

I deliver many things near and far.     pilot

I can stop traffic with one hand.     truck driver

I grow things to eat.     fisherman

I fly airplanes.     baker

I bake cakes and cookies.     police officer

**Day 10** Find the hidden picture. Color the long i (ī) words in blue and the short i (ĭ) words green. (The sound of (ī) can be in words with the letter y, too.)

| bib | fry | tie | light | my | sigh | try | wig |
|-----|-----|-----|-------|-----|------|-----|-----|
| six | bike | sign | pie | guy | by | high | if |
| fib | gift | pit | dry | bite | miss | fish | lit |
| chin | sit | pill | time | night | hid | bill | quit |
| bin | mit | tin | cry | dime | win | fit | will |
| pin | fine | lie | sight | why | right | shy | fin |
| zip | ride | buy | side | hike | kite | nine | did |

**Something is wrong with one word in each sentence. Find the word and correct it!**

1. Allie bocked a cake.

2. Denise and i went to the zoo.

3. grayson has a train.

4. Clean your toy rom.

5. Rob will do hiz devotions.

© Summer Bridge Activities™ 1–2    22    www.summerbrains.com

**Complete the number families.**

**James Russell Lowell:** Reputation is ... the light by which the world looks for and finds merit.

**Day 11**

2, 3, 5

2, 7, 9

3, 5, 8

2 + 3 = ☐          7 + 2 = ☐          5 + 3 = ☐

3 + ☐ = 5          ☐ + 7 = 9          ☐ + ☐ = 8

5 − 2 = ☐          9 − ☐ = 2          8 − ☐ = ☐

☐ − 3 = 2          9 − ☐ = 7          ☐ − 3 = ☐

**Circle the largest number in each set.**

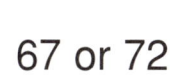

17 or 71          91 or 19          67 or 72

34 or 30          26 or 41          29 or 40

**Read each puzzle. On the line, write a word that rhymes with the underlined word.**

1. It rhymes with <u>mat</u>.
   It is a good pet.
   It is a
   _____
   ------------------
   _____

2. It rhymes with <u>boys</u>.
   Kids love to play with them. They are
   _____
   ------------------

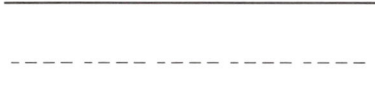

**Day 11** Match the words to the right contraction.

EXAMPLE:

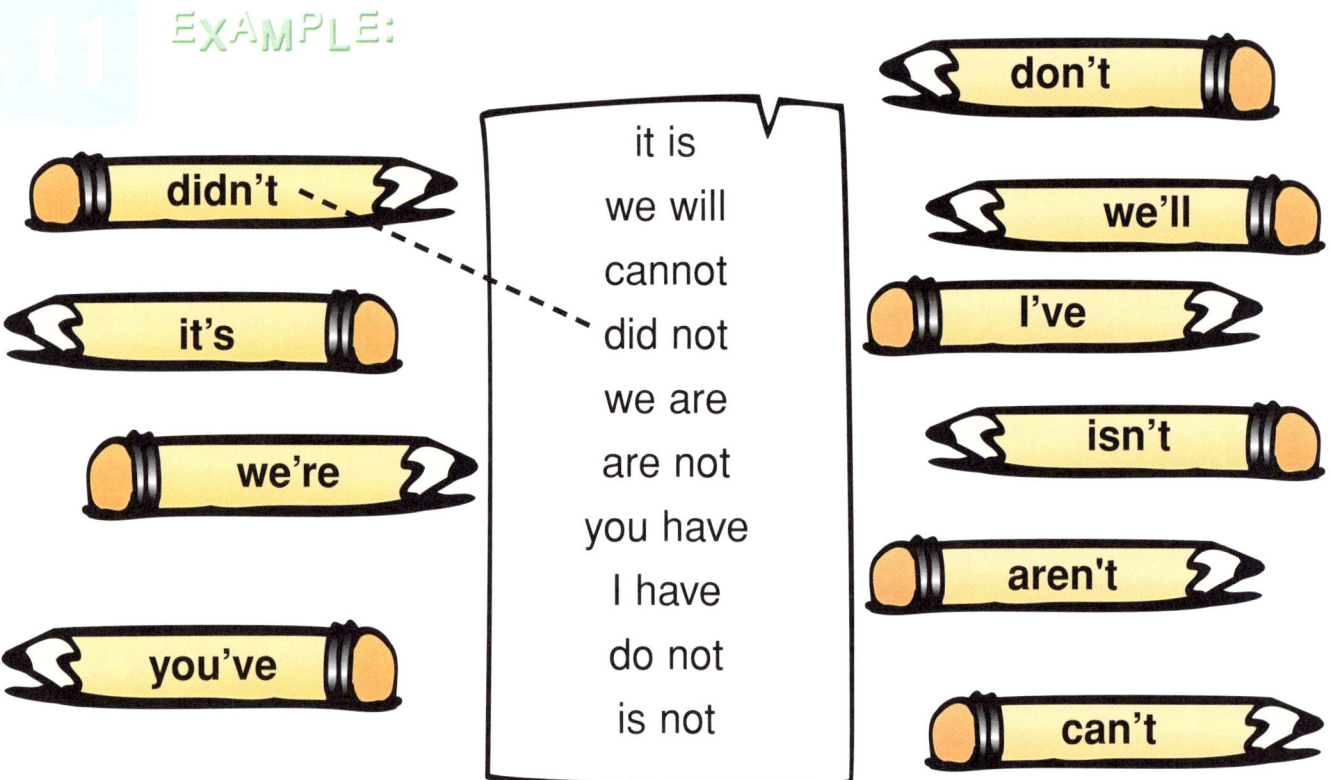

**Unscramble the sentences.**

1. swim like Ducks to.

2. pigs mud Do play in the?

3. nests Birds in trees make.

4. fun today Are having you?

Add or subtract.

**Psalm 118:8**
It is better to take refuge in the LORD than to trust in man.

# Day 12

8 + 2 = ____   10 - 4 = ____   2 + 1 = ____
4 + 4 = ____   5 - 2 = ____    7 - 3 = ____
3 + 7 = ____   6 - 3 = ____    5 - 4 = ____
1 + 9 = ____   4 - 4 = ____    10 - 5 = ____
3 + 3 = ____   7 - 4 = ____    3 + 2 = ____
6 + 4 = ____   3 - 1 = ____    5 + 4 = ____
5 + 2 = ____   9 - 4 = ____    6 - 2 = ____
10 + 0 = ____  8 - 3 = ____    4 + 4 = ____

**Blends are two different consonants which join together to make a certain sound. Write the blends for the pictures below.**

EXAMPLE:

d  r    ___ ___   ___ ___   ___ ___

___ ___   ___ ___   ___ ___   ___ ___

**Day 12** Match the contractions with the word pairs. Write the answer on the line.

Read the word on each balloon. If the word has a long u (ū) sound, color the balloon yellow. If the word doesn't have a long u (ū) sound, color the balloon any color but yellow.

Circle each problem that equals the number at the start of each row.

**Psalm 119:11**
I have hidden your word in my heart that I might not sin against you.

**Day 13**

EXAMPLE:

| 7 | (3 + 4) | (9 - 2) | (5 + 2) | 7 - 2 | 6 - 4 | (7 + 0) | (8 - 1) |
|---|---|---|---|---|---|---|---|
| 5 | 6 - 1 | 0 + 5 | 4 + 1 | 9 - 4 | 10 - 5 | 8 + 2 | 7 - 2 |
| 4 | 3 + 1 | 5 - 2 | 6 + 3 | 10 - 6 | 9 - 5 | 2 + 2 | 8 - 4 |
| 8 | 10 - 2 | 2 + 6 | 9 - 1 | 8 - 0 | 3 + 5 | 7 + 2 | 1 + 7 |
| 3 | 5 - 4 | 2 + 1 | 6 - 3 | 9 - 6 | 0 + 3 | 9 - 2 | 7 - 4 |
| 6 | 12 - 6 | 6 + 5 | 5 + 1 | 10 - 4 | 8 - 3 | 4 + 2 | 7 - 1 |

Find and circle the following words.

| boy | bay | enjoy | say |
| joy | hay | toy | day |

| d | f | b | o | y | b | h | g | e |
|---|---|---|---|---|---|---|---|---|
| a | l | e | d | c | p | a | h | n |
| y | m | k | b | q | r | y | i | j |
| o | n | q | a | t | t | s | j | o |
| r | s | a | y | j | o | y | v | y |
| s | w | x | u | c | y | f | g | z |

**Day 13**

Combine the word and the picture to form a compound word. Write it in the blank.

EXAMPLE:

1. cook +  = __cookbook__

2. base +  = _____

3.  + bell = _____

4. life +  = _____

5.  + fighter = _____

6. cat +  = _____

Put a 1, 2, or 3 in each box to show the right order.

☐ Allie ran into a rock with her bike.

☐ Allie and her bike tipped over.

☐ Allie went for a bike ride.

☐ Rob woke up and got out of bed.

☐ Rob rode the bus to school.

☐ Rob said the blessing and ate a big breakfast.

Complete the number families.

**Proverbs 3:5**
Trust in the LORD with all your heart and lean not on your own understanding.

**Day 14**

**4, 9, 5**

4 + 5 = ___
5 + 4 = ___
9 − 5 = ___
9 − 4 = ___

**6, 2, 8**

6 + ___ = 8
2 + ___ = ___
8 − ___ = 2
8 − ___ = ___

**3, 7, 10**

___ + ___ = ___
___ + ___ = ___
___ − ___ = ___
___ − ___ = ___

Write the beginning and ending sounds.

___ e ___
___ u ___
___ u ___
___ a ___
___ e ___
___ i ___
___ o ___
___ i ___

**Day 14**

Circle the sentence that goes with the picture.

1. Allie walked up the stairs.
2. Allie walked down the stairs.
3. Allie sat on the stairs.

1. Rob threw the baseball to his dad.
2. Rob threw the baseball to Denise.
3. Rob threw the baseball to his mom.

Are the underlined words telling who, what, when, or where? Write the answer at the beginning of each sentence.

EXAMPLE:

___who___ 1. My mother is going home.

_____ 2. We will go swimming tomorrow morning.

_____ 3. Children like to eat candy.

_____ 4. The ball is under the bed.

_____ 5. On the Fourth of July, my family and I will go on a picnic.

_____ 6. A big truck was stuck in the mud.

_____ 7. Denise and her friend went on a trip.

_____ 8. The boy lost his new skates at the park.

_____ 9. The clown made everyone laugh.

Read and answer the math problems below. Write each problem.

**Proverbs 17:17**
A friend loves at all times, and a brother is born for adversity.

# Day 15

1. The shepherd found four lost sheep the first night. He found six lost sheep the second night. How many sheep did he find?

   _____ + _____ = _____

2. Rob had three balls. He found three more. How many balls does he have in all?

   _____ + _____ = _____

3. A farmer had nine cows. He sold five of them. How many cows does he have left?

   _____ - _____ = _____

---

**Write the correct color words.**

Snow is _____.
Grapes are _____.
The lettuce is _____.
The sun is _____.
My hat is _____.
Sam's dog is _____.
My friend's house is _____.
Tomatoes are _____.
Chocolate candy is _____.
Marshmallows are _____.

Teddy bears are _____.
The sky is _____.
Trees are _____.
My shoes are _____.
My eyes are _____.
My hair is _____.
Mud is _____.
Goldfish are _____.
Blackboards are _____.
Dad's car is _____.

# Day 15

Find and circle the words with the long u (ū) vowel sound.

| use | huge | glue | music |
| cube | cute | salute | tune |

| g | l | u | e | l | s | q | t | m |
|---|---|---|---|---|---|---|---|---|
| c | a | s | f | r | a | b | u | u |
| u | o | e | h | t | l | m | n | s |
| t | d | n | c | h | u | g | e | i |
| e | j | s | u | k | t | p | v | c |
| i | w | c | u | b | e | x | e | g |

Check the box which best describes the picture.

☐ The mouse is in the box.

☐ The mouse is under the box.

☐ The mouse jumped out of the box.

☐ The bird is sleeping.

☐ The bird loves to sing.

☐ The bird never sings.

© Summer Bridge Activities™ 1–2          www.summerbrains.com

# Words to Sound, Read, and Spell

### short ă words
| | |
|---|---|
| can | mad |
| cap | gas |
| fan | sad |
| lap | ax |
| man | bag |
| map | tax |
| ran | rag |
| nap | wax |
| bad | tag |
| tap | cab |
| dad | wag |
| yap | jab |
| had | gag |
| has | nab |

### short ĕ words
| | |
|---|---|
| bet | fed |
| beg | vet |
| get | led |
| leg | set |
| jet | wed |
| peg | wet |
| let | hen |
| hem | yet |
| met | pen |
| pep | ten |
| net | |
| web | |
| bed | |
| yes | |

### short ĭ words
| | |
|---|---|
| bit | him |
| bib | hip |
| fit | rim |
| rib | lip |
| mitt | bid |
| fib | sip |
| hit | hid |
| mix | rip |
| pit | kid |
| six | tip |
| quit | lid |
| fix | zip |
| sit | did |
| dim | quip |
| dip | rid |

### short ŏ words
| | |
|---|---|
| dog | pop |
| ox | hot |
| fog | rod |
| box | lot |
| log | pod |
| fox | tot |
| jog | cot |
| mob | dot |
| hop | not |
| rob | got |
| mop | pot |
| sob | |
| top | |
| job | |

### short ŭ words
| | |
|---|---|
| bug | sum |
| rut | rug |
| dug | gum |
| bun | tug |
| hug | bus |
| fun | lug |
| jug | tub |
| run | but |
| mud | sub |
| sun | cut |
| dud | rub |
| cup | nut |
| hum | cub |
| pup | |
| mum | |
| mug | |

### -ll words
| | |
|---|---|
| bill | tell |
| fill | well |
| dill | yell |
| hill | bell |
| spill | fell |
| will | dull |
| quill | doll |
| sell | |

### -ss words
| | |
|---|---|
| pass | kiss |
| mass | miss |
| boss | bliss |
| moss | fuss |
| toss | muss |
| loss | less |
| hiss | mess |

### -ck words
| | |
|---|---|
| back | peck |
| pack | duck |
| dock | deck |
| quack | luck |
| lock | kick |
| rack | tuck |
| sock | lick |
| tack | pick |
| rock | sick |
| neck | quick |
| buck | wick |

### -ff words
| | |
|---|---|
| buff | huff |
| cuff | puff |

## L- Blends to Read!

### fl-
flat, flag, flap, fled, flex, flick, flip, flock, floss, flop, fluff, flux

### sl-
slab, slack, slam, slap, sled, slick, slid, slim, slip, slot, slug

### cl-
class, clap, clam, click, cliff, clip, clock, clog, club, cluck

### pl-
plan, plat, pled, plot, plop, pluck, plum, plug, plus

### bl-
black, bled, bless, bliss, blob, block, blot, bluff

### gl-
glum, glut, gloss, glass, glad, glory, glow

## R- Blends to Read!

### gr-
grab, grape, grass, grid, grim, grin, grill, grip, grog, grub, gruff

### br-
brag, brake, brand, brass, brave, brick

### fr-
free, fret, frill, frog, from, fry

### dr-
drag, drab, dress, drill, drip, drop, drug, drum

### tr-
track, trap, trick, trip, trim, trot, truck

### cr-
crab, crack, crib, crick, cross, crop

### pr-
press, price, prince, print, prize, proof

## Look at the endings.

| _-mp_ | | _-st_ | | | _-sk_ | _-sp_ | _-lf_ | _-lk_ | _-lp_ | _-lt_ |
|---|---|---|---|---|---|---|---|---|---|---|
| camp | romp | cast | rest | dust | mask | gasp | shelf | milk | scalp | belt |
| lamp | chomp | best | fist | must | task | clasp | golf | silk | help | melt |
| ramp | | fast | test | mist | disk | lisp | | bulk | gulp | spilt |
| stamp | | nest | lost | | brisk | crisp | | sulk | pulp | quilt |
| limp | | last | vest | | dusk | | | elk | | |
| stomp | | pest | cost | | tusk | | | | | |
| bump | | past | zest | | desk | | | | | |
| dump | | jest | frost | | | | | | | |
| jump | | blast | chest | | | | | | | |
| pump | | quest | bust | | | | | | | |
| stump | | list | last | | | | | | | |

## Two sounds of _oo_!

| 1 | 2 | | |
|---|---|---|---|
| book | boo | doom | goose |
| look | moo | broom | moose |
| took | too | bloom | loose |
| shook | zoo | groom | boot |
| hook | moon | gloom | hoot |
| cook | soon | cool | loot |
| crook | noon | fool | root |
| brook | spoon | tool | toot |
| hood | food | pool | scoot |
| wood | spook | spool | hoop |
| hoof | boom | stool | loop |
| stood | room | school | |
| foot | zoom | ooze | |
| wool | | | |

## Try these!

| _st-_ | _sp-_ | _sn-_ | _sk-_ | _sm-_ | _sw-_ |
|---|---|---|---|---|---|
| stick | spud | snug | skip | smack | swag |
| stiff | spun | snub | skid | smell | swam |
| still | speck | snob | skit | smock | swim |
| stop | spell | sniff | skill | smog | Swiss |
| stock | sped | snip | skim | smug | swig |
| stab | span | snack | | | swell |
| stack | spat | snap | | | |
| staff | spill | | | | |
| stag | spin | | | | |
| stem | split | | | | |
| step | | | | | |

## These vowels go walking and the first one does the talking!

| | | | |
|---|---|---|---|
| oat | oak | toaster | blackboard |
| boat | soak | toast | dashboard |
| coat | cloak | coach | surfboard |
| float | croak | poach | skateboard |
| throat | soap | approach | scoreboard |
| load | oar | cockroach | steamboat |
| toad | roar | raincoat | railroad |
| road | foal | coatrack | roadrunner |
| roam | coal | foam | boast |
| moan | coast | groan | roast |

### Summer Bridge Activities™ for Young Christians
# Motivational Calendar!

Month _____

My parents and I decided that if I complete 20 days of *Summer Bridge Activities*™ *for Young Christians* and read _____ minutes a day, my incentive/reward will be:

_____

Child's Signature _____ Parent's Signature _____

| | | |
|---|---|---|
| Day 1  ☆ 🕊 📕 _____ | Day 11 ☆ 🕊 📕 _____ |
| Day 2  ☆ 🕊 📕 _____ | Day 12 ☆ 🕊 📕 _____ |
| Day 3  ☆ 🕊 📕 _____ | Day 13 ☆ 🕊 📕 _____ |
| Day 4  ☆ 🕊 📕 _____ | Day 14 ☆ 🕊 📕 _____ |
| Day 5  ☆ 🕊 📕 _____ | Day 15 ☆ 🕊 📕 _____ |
| Day 6  ☆ 🕊 📕 _____ | Day 16 ☆ 🕊 📕 _____ |
| Day 7  ☆ 🕊 📕 _____ | Day 17 ☆ 🕊 📕 _____ |
| Day 8  ☆ 🕊 📕 _____ | Day 18 ☆ 🕊 📕 _____ |
| Day 9  ☆ 🕊 📕 _____ | Day 19 ☆ 🕊 📕 _____ |
| Day 10 ☆ 🕊 📕 _____ | Day 20 ☆ 🕊 📕 _____ |

**Child:** Color the ☆ for daily activities completed.
Color the 🕊 for daily devotionals completed.
Color the 📕 for daily reading completed.
**Parent:** Initial the ___ when your child is complete.

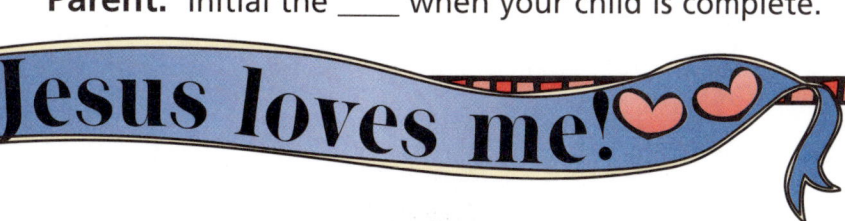

**Fun Activity Ideas to Go Along with the Second Section!**

1. Decorate your bike. Have a neighborhood parade.
2. Catch a butterfly.
3. Get the neighborhood together and play hide-and-seek.
4. Take a tour of the local hospital.
5. Check on how your garden is doing.
6. Make snow cones with crushed ice and punch.
7. Go on a bike ride.
8. Run through the sprinklers.
9. Create a family symphony with bottles, pans, and rubber bands.
10. Collect sticks and mud. Build a bird's nest.
11. Help plan your family grocery list.
12. Go swimming with a friend.
13. Clean your bedroom and closet.
14. Go to the local zoo.
15. In the early morning, listen to the birds sing.
16. Make a cereal treat.
17. Read a story to a younger child.
18. Lie down on the grass and find shapes in the clouds.
19. Color noodles with food coloring. String them for a necklace or glue a design on paper.
20. Organize your toys.

**Complete the counting patterns.**

**Oliver Wendell Holmes:** Every calling is great when greatly pursued.

**Day 1**

| 10 | 20 |  | 40 |  |  | 70 |  |  | 100 |

| 5 | 10 | 15 |  |  |  | 35 | 40 |  |  |
|---|----|----|--|--|--|----|----|--|--|
| 55 |  | 70 |  |  |  | 90 |  |  |  |

| 2 | 4 |  | 8 |  | 12 |  |  | 18 |  | 22 |
|---|---|--|---|--|----|--|--|----|--|----|
|  | 26 |  | 32 |  |  |  |  | 42 |  |  |

**Write the short and long vowels.**

EXAMPLE: r_a_ke

t____be

b____x

d____ck

t____re

l____mp

m____lk

t____e

# Day 1

**Hobbies.**

A hobby is something we enjoy doing in our spare time. Some children like to make things. Some like to collect things. Some play music, and some children do other things. Hobbies are fun. Do you have a hobby?

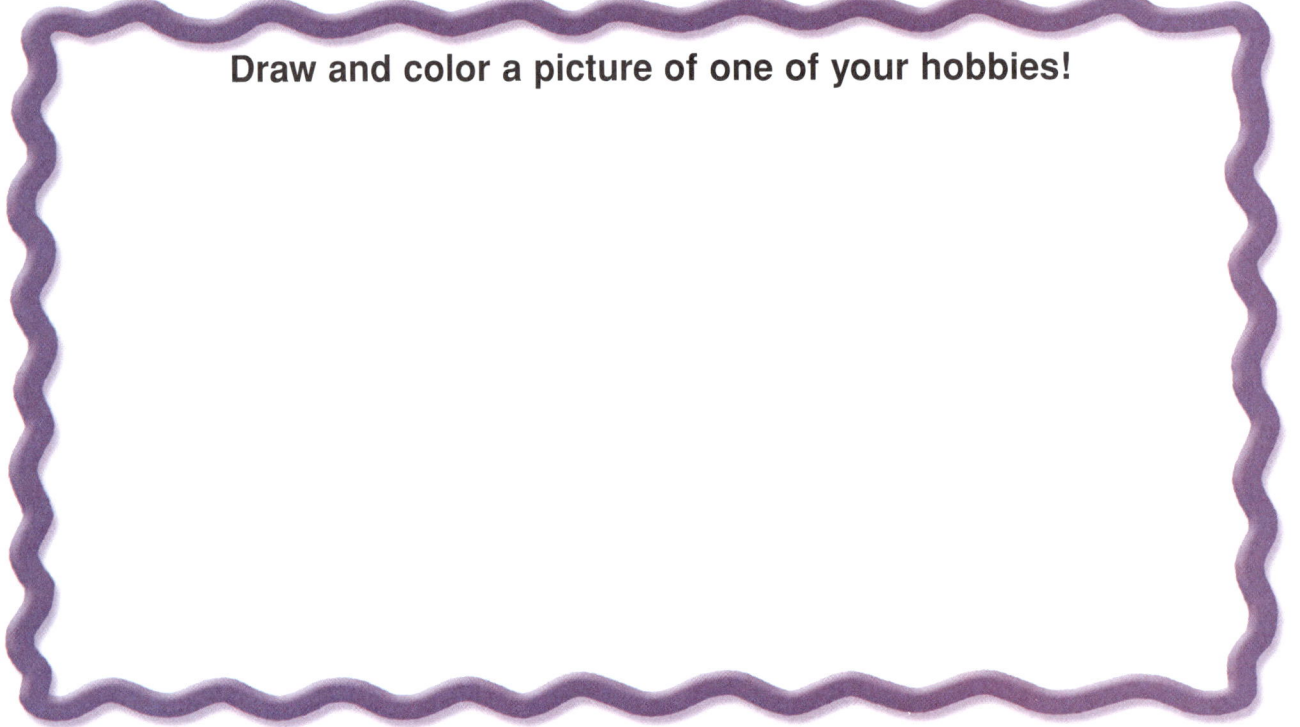

**Draw and color a picture of one of your hobbies!**

**Catch each butterfly. Put each one in the right net by drawing a line to where it belongs.**

EXAMPLE:

**Decide how many tens and how many ones make up each number.**

**Isaiah 45:22**
"Turn to me and be saved, all you ends of the earth; for I am God, and there is no other."

**Day 2**

EXAMPLE: 1s 10s

26 = __2__ tens __6__ ones     41 = _____ ones _____ tens
45 = _____ tens _____ ones     69 = _____ ones _____ tens
65 = _____ ones _____ tens     84 = _____ tens _____ ones
17 = _____ ones _____ tens     72 = _____ ones _____ tens
50 = _____ tens _____ ones     39 = _____ tens _____ ones
97 = _____ ones _____ tens     51 = _____ ones _____ tens
35 = _____ tens _____ ones     100 = _____ tens _____ ones

Read the sentence; then follow the directions.

# Denise hugged her dog three times.

1. Circle the word <u>hugged</u>.
2. Draw a box around the word that tells who Denise hugged.
3. Underline the word that tells who hugged the dog.
4. Draw a picture of Denise and her dog.

# Day 2

**Number these sentences in the order they happened.**

☐ The sun came out. It was a pretty day.

☐ The thunder roared, and the lightning flashed.

☐ It rained and rained.

☐ Allie put her umbrella away.

☐ Allie walked under her umbrella.

☐ The clouds came, and the sky was dark.

**Finish the story.**

**Once there was a sun. The happy sun loved to shine its bright rays onto the earth because...**

_____
_____
_____
_____
_____
_____
_____
_____

© Summer Bridge Activities™ 1–2    www.summerbrains.com

Draw the hands to match the time, or write the time to match the hands.

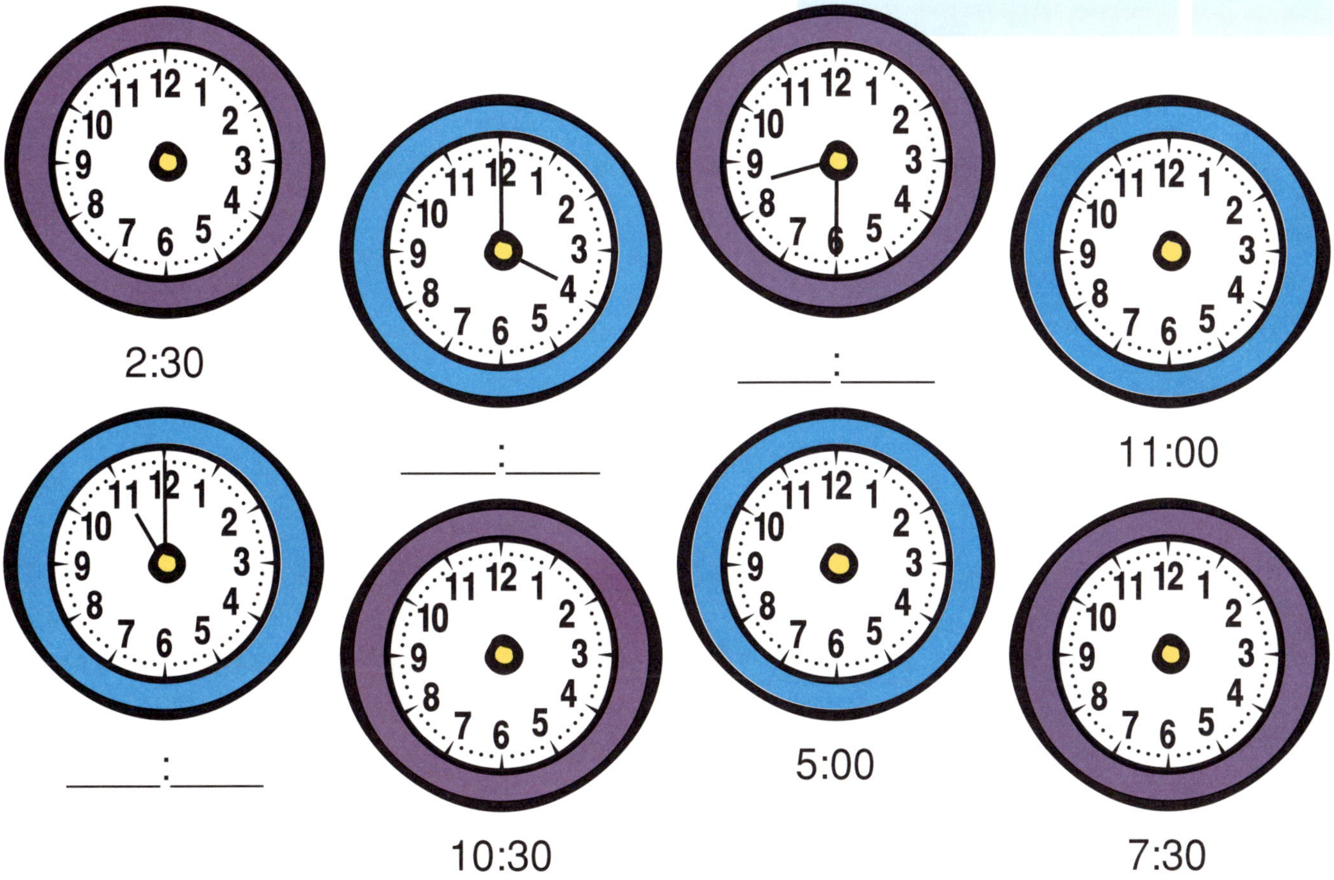

**Saint Augustine:** He who is filled with love is filled with God himself.

**Day 3**

2:30

____:____

____:____

11:00

____:____

10:30

5:00

7:30

Circle the letters that spell the beginning sound of each picture.

# Day 3

**Read and decide.**

One day, a man went on a hunt. He hunted for a long time. At the end of the day, he was very happy. What do you think the man found? Did he find something to eat? Did he find something pretty? Did he find something funny? Decide what the man found and draw a picture of it!

---

**Put the following words in alphabetical order.**

he
up
fat
little
big
stop
and
out
slow
go

1. _____
2. _____
3. _____
4. _____
5. _____
6. _____
7. _____
8. _____
9. _____
10. _____

**Solve these problems.**

1. Rob found five bees. Denise found five bees. How many bees are there in all?

   _____ bees

2. Lori has four fish. Matt has six fish. How many fish are there in all?

   _____ fish

> **Matthew 5:16**
> [L]et your light shine before men, that they may see your good deeds and praise your Father in heaven.

**Day 4**

---

| Word Study and Spelling List |       |
|------------------------------|-------|
| dime                         | make  |
| name                         | plate |
| gave                         | size  |
| nine                         | five  |
| lake                         | bake  |
| time                         | wise  |

**Write the words with the long a (ā) sound.**

**Write the words with the long i (ī) sound.**

**Day** Read each story. Choose the best title.

Tanner is up now. He hits the ball. "Run, Tanner, run! Run to first base, then to second. Can you run to home base?"

1. Running  2. Tanner Plays  3. Tanner's Baseball Game

A rabbit can jump. Frogs can jump too—but a kangaroo is the best jumper of all!

1. Jumping Rabbits
2. Animals That Jump
3. Hop! Hop! Hop!

God was going to send a flood. So Noah built an ark. He loaded it with many animals.

1. Rain, Rain, Go Away
2. The Long Day
3. Getting Ready for the Flood

Rob gave his pet dog a bone. He gave his fat cat some canned cat food. He also fed the ducks.

1. Feeding the Animals
2. Rob's Animals
3. Cats, Dogs, and Birds

Make these words plural, meaning more than one, by adding **-s** or **-es**.

EXAMPLE:
1. cat  **cats**
2. glass  _____
3. truck  _____
4. fan  _____
5. wish  _____
6. ball  _____
7. box  _____
8. bird  _____

9. kitten  _____
10. inch  _____
11. dish  _____
12. clock  _____
13. bus  _____
14. peach  _____
15. brush  _____
16. dog  _____

Subtract and fill in the answers on the outer circle.

**Matthew 6:11**
Give us today our daily bread.

**Day 5**

EXAMPLE:

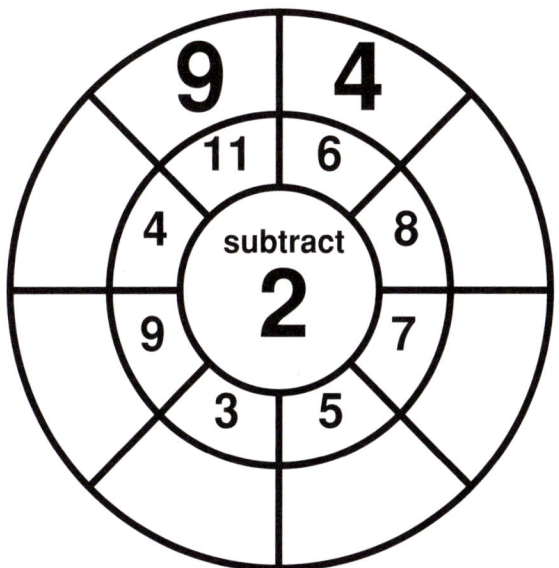

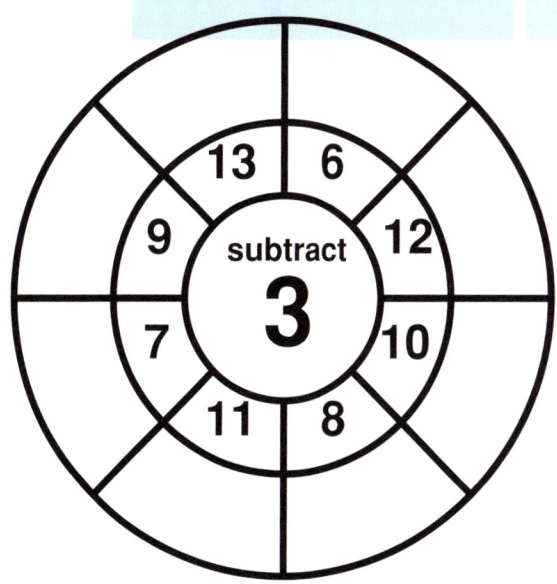

Circle and write the word that goes with each picture.

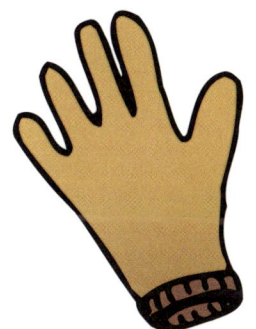

glove  _____

glue   _____

flower _____

flag   _____

flashlight _____

fly       _____

# Day 5

Use the following words to fill in the blanks:

Who    What    Where    Why    When

1. _____ are my keys?

2. _____ funny toy is mine?

3. _____ is your birthday party?

4. _____ is Mother coming?

5. _____ was there?

6. _____ is the sky dark?

Draw the other half. Color.

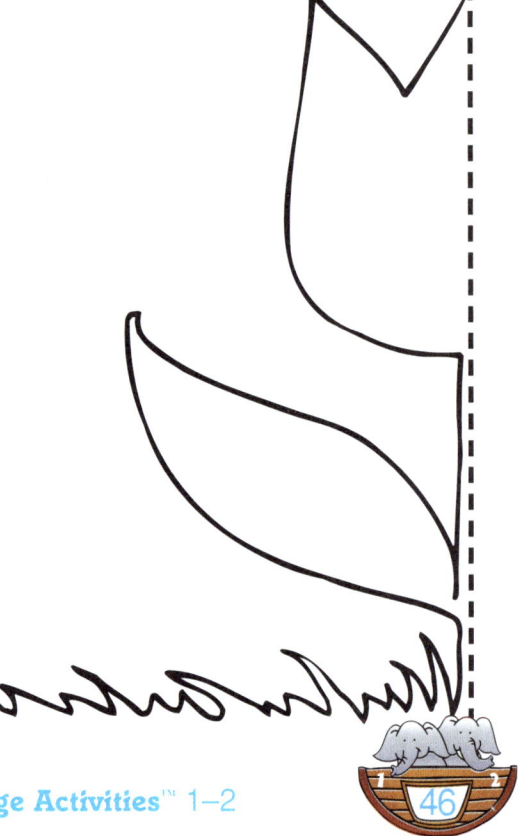

Solve the following problems.

**Mother Teresa:** If you judge people, you have no time to love them.

# Day 6

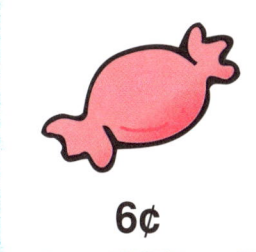 6¢    11¢    5¢    9¢

**EXAMPLE:**
Lori has 15¢. She bought an

```
  15
-  9
-----
  6¢
```

How much does she have left?

Grayson bought a  and a
How much did he spend?

Allie has 12¢. She bought a

How much does she have left?

Tanner bought a  and a
How much did he spend?

**What month comes next? Fill in the blanks.**

| January | February | |
|---------|----------|---------|
| April | | June |
| | | September |
| | November | |

How many months are in a year? _____

# Day 6

Write the correct word on each line.

1. Rob has a sore _____.
   **thirst**   **throat**   **thunder**

2. May I please have _____ balls?
   **three**   **third**   **fifth**

3. My little _____ is three years old.
   **mother**   **father**   **brother**

4. We could walk _____.
   **together**   **rather**   **other**

5. You need to _____ fast.
   **third**   **thank**   **think**

Finish the story.

Last night I had the strangest dream. I dreamed that I…

**Day 7**

Do a survey with your family and friends to see which flavor of popsicle is the most popular.

> **Matthew 7:7**
> "Ask and it will be given to you; seek and you will find; knock and the door will be opened to you."

_____ root beer　　_____ lime
_____ orange　　_____ cherry
_____ banana　　_____ grape
_____ (others not listed)

Graph the results of your survey by placing an X on the coordinates of the number of people who liked each flavor.

| | 1 | 2 | 3 | 4 | 5 | 6 | 7 | 8 | 9 | 10 | 11 | 12 | 13 | 14 | 15 | 16 | 17 | 18 | 19 | 20 |
|---|---|---|---|---|---|---|---|---|---|---|---|---|---|---|---|---|---|---|---|---|
| Root Beer | | | | | | | | | | | | | | | | | | | | |
| Orange | | | | | | | | | | | | | | | | | | | | |
| Banana | | | | | | | | | | | | | | | | | | | | |
| Lime | | | | | | | | | | | | | | | | | | | | |
| Cherry | | | | | | | | | | | | | | | | | | | | |
| Grape | | | | | | | | | | | | | | | | | | | | |
| Other | | | | | | | | | | | | | | | | | | | | |

What is your favorite flavor?　　Which flavor was the least popular?

_____　　_____

Which flavor was the most popular?

_____

**Read, study, and spell.**

| | | | | | |
|---|---|---|---|---|---|
| 1. | bake | bakes | baking | baked | baker |
| 2. | walk | walks | walking | walked | walker |
| 3. | stop | stops | stopping | stopped | stopper |
| 4. | mix | mixes | mixing | mixed | mixer |
| 5. | listen | listens | listening | listened | listener |
| 6. | pray | prays | praying | prayed | prayer |
| 7. | call | calls | calling | called | caller |
| 8. | hug | hugs | hugging | hugged | hugger |

www.summerbrains.com　　© Summer Bridge Activities™ 1–2

**Day 7**

**Read the story; then answer the questions below.**

Mike lives on a farm. He wakes up early to do chores. Mike feeds the horses and pigs. He also collects the eggs. Sometimes, he helps his dad milk the cows. His favorite thing to do in the morning is eat breakfast.

1. Where does Mike live? _____
2. Why does he have to wake up early? _____
3. Name one chore Mike has to do: _____
4. What is his favorite thing to do in the morning?
_____

**Fill in the letters under the picture. Write the words on the correct line. Answer the puzzle below. Color each picture the color below its line.**

# oi

c____ ____n      v____ ____ce      ____ ____l

_____ You can put this in your pocket.
**yellow**

_____ You use this to hum, talk, and laugh.
**green**

_____ Put this on and no more squeaks!
**red**

**Add.**

**Matthew 21:22**
"If you believe, you will receive whatever you ask for in prayer."

**Day 8**

1.  
```
  2    1    4    5    2    4    5    3    8
  2    1    4    5    3    3    4    5    0
 +2   +1   +4   +5   +2   +0   +5   +3   +2
```

2.  
```
  3    6    7   10    8    5    9    2    4
  3    6    0   10    3    1    0    3    4
 +3   +6   +7  +10   +2   +5   +1   +7   +3
```

**Give some facts about you and your family. Draw a picture of your family.**

1. I live in _____.
2. I have _____ sisters.
3. I have _____ brothers.
4. My mom's name is _____.
5. My dad's name is _____.
6. This summer we are going to _____.
7. I am _____ years old.
8. We have a pet _____.
9. My favorite food is _____.
10. My favorite Bible story is _____.

# Day 8

**What day comes next? Fill in the blanks.**

Sunday, _____, _____, Wednesday, _____, Friday, and _____.

How many days are in a week? _____

Name the days you go to school during the week.

_____, _____, _____, _____, _____

---

**Complete these sentences by unscrambling the words and writing them in the blanks.**

1. Matt had a _____ for _____ mother.
               **igft**            **ihs**

2. The _____ has a broken window.
        **acr**

3. A bee _____ on _____ flower.
         **ats**        **hte**

4. My _____ works at the _____.
       **add**           **tsoer**

5. Sue _____ a _____ dog named Spot.
       **sha**     **ept**

**Add.**

| 5 | 8 | 3 | 9 | 15 | 10 | 8 | 9 | 6 |
|---|---|---|---|----|----|---|---|---|
| +7 | +4 | +7 | +5 | +2 | +6 | +3 | +4 | +5 |

**Subtract.**

| 12 | 9 | 11 | 8 | 10 | 6 | 7 | 12 | 10 |
|----|---|----|---|----|---|---|----|----|
| -8 | -4 | -7 | -8 | -2 | -2 | -5 | -4 | -6 |

**Samuel Smiles:** Men who are resolved to find a way for themselves will always find opportunities enough.

**Day 9**

Write the words that match the clues.

EXAMPLE:

1. It begins like <u>stuck</u>. It rhymes with <u>late</u>.
   **state**

2. It begins like <u>rip</u>. It rhymes with <u>cake</u>.
   _____

3. It begins like <u>very</u>. It rhymes with <u>note</u>. _____

4. It begins like <u>break</u>. It rhymes with <u>him</u>. _____

5. It begins like <u>gum</u>. It rhymes with <u>late</u>. _____

6. It begins like <u>trip</u>. It rhymes with <u>rim</u>. _____

# Day 9

**Read the story below and then answer the questions.**

Denise has a box of peaches. She wants to take the peaches home to her mother, so her mother can make a peach pie. Denise says, "I love to eat peach pie!"

1. Who has a box of peaches? _____
2. Who does she want to take the peaches to? _____
3. What does she want her mother to make? _____
4. Denise says, "I love to eat _____!"

---

**Complete the phrase below. Write at least three complete sentences.**

I like myself because I can…

_____
_____
_____
_____
_____
_____
_____
_____
_____
_____

Write the numeral by the number word.

**Luke 1:37**
"For nothing is impossible with God."

# Day 10

_____ six        _____ nine       _____ four       _____ seven
_____ ten        _____ two        _____ three      _____ one
_____ five       _____ eight      _____ zero       _____ twelve

_____ nineteen          _____ eleven            _____ fourteen
_____ twenty-one        _____ sixteen           _____ eighteen
_____ thirteen          _____ fifteen           _____ seventeen
_____ twenty            _____ twenty-five       _____ thirty

---

Does the **y** say (ī) or (ē) in the words below? Write **i** or **e** in the boxes.

**ī or ē**

EXAMPLE:

| ē | | | | | |
|---|---|---|---|---|---|
| baby | fly | windy | bunny | fry | cherry |

| | | | | | |
|---|---|---|---|---|---|
| shy | family | silly | happy | jelly | pony |

| | | | | | |
|---|---|---|---|---|---|
| cry | my | funny | buy | try | candy |

# Day 10

**Draw the following.**

1. Draw one tree.
2. Draw four flowers.
3. Color one orange butterfly in the tree.
4. Draw a park bench.
5. Draw three pigeons beside the bench.
6. Draw a yellow sun.

**Read the story; then answer the questions.**

Rob is excited for summer. He wants to do many things. He wants to visit all of the animals at the zoo. He also wants to go camping in the mountains. Rob loves to swim and play with his friends, too.

1. What is Rob excited for? _____
2. What does he want to visit at the zoo? _____
3. Where does he want to go camping? _____
4. What does Rob love to do? _____
   and _____

**Luke 10:27**
"Love the Lord your God with all your heart and with all your soul and with all your strength and with all your mind."

# Day 11

Use the problems below to work on place value. Be sure to read before you write.

46 = _____ tens _____ ones
19 = _____ ones _____ tens
84 = _____ tens _____ ones
64 = _____ tens _____ ones
7 tens and 6 ones = _____
4 tens and 0 ones = _____
1 ten and 1 one = _____
9 ones and 3 tens = _____
1 hundred, 2 tens, and 8 ones = _____

Circle the root, or base, word in each of the following words.

EXAMPLE:
1. (ru)nning
2. hopped
3. fastest
4. standing
5. ripped
6. tallest
7. digging
8. slowly
9. faithful
10. boxes
11. lovely
12. sickness
13. stepping
14. careful
15. dropped
16. catches
17. heavenly
18. rabbits
19. starry
20. mopped
21. sadness
22. missing
23. bigger
24. mixed

**Day 11**

Fill in the circle in front of each correct answer. There may be more than one correct answer in each box.

**We can smell**
○ cakes in the oven.
○ cookies on a plate.
○ wind blowing the trees.

**We can feel**
○ the cold rain.
○ sand on the seashore.
○ the night.

**We can see**
○ a sweater on the shelf.
○ a pain in our leg.
○ a watch on a chain.

**We can taste**
○ the porch swing.
○ a green apple.
○ a cheese sandwich.

**We can feel**
○ the hot sunshine.
○ a cold dish.
○ the dog chasing a cat.

**We can see**
○ soldiers marching.
○ the weeks.
○ a scratch on the table.

**We can taste**
○ a dill pickle.
○ popcorn in a dish.
○ a cloud in the sky.

**We can smell**
○ a rose on a bush.
○ the ticking of a clock.
○ dinner cooking.

If you planted a garden, what would you plant and why? Draw a picture.

**Solve these problems.**

**John 3:16**
"For God so loved the world that he gave his one and only Son, that whoever believes in him shall ... have eternal life."

**Day 12**

Tanner spent 8¢. Denise spent 2¢. How much did they spend altogether?

Allie has 10 bows. Lori has 5 bows. How many bows do they have?

Rob has 6 fish. Matt has 2 fish. How many fish do they have in all?

Grayson has 3 balloons. Matt has 8 balloons. How many balloons do they have in all?

**Study and spell the words in this word list.**

| brave | glad | stone | fast | crop | lost |
|-------|------|-------|------|------|------|
| slip | slap | last | step | stop | list |

**Unscramble the words.** (Clue: You will find them in your word list.)

psla _____   etsno _____   stal _____

ptos _____   rebav _____   solt _____

porc _____   lgda _____   atsf _____

psil _____   epst _____   stil _____

**Day 12**

Read each paragraph and circle the sentence that explains the main idea of the paragraph.

1. Allie's umbrella is old. It has holes in it. The color is faded. It doesn't keep the rain off her.

2. Tabby is a tan and white cat. He has a long, white tail. He lives on a farm in the country. Tabby helps the farmer by catching mice in the barn. He sleeps on soft, green hay.

3. There are big, black clouds in the sky. The wind is blowing, and it is getting cold. It is going to snow.

**Find the opposites in the word search box.**

1. The opposite of clean is _____.
2. The opposite of night is _____.
3. The opposite of hot is _____.
4. The opposite of light is _____.
5. The opposite of laugh is _____.
6. The opposite of up is _____.

| v | d | i | r | t | y | e | h | k |
|---|---|---|---|---|---|---|---|---|
| a | b | a | m | c | e | u | d | g |
| x | c | r | y | o | d | s | a | j |
| w | l | h | o | l | r | j | y | n |
| q | a | z | c | d | d | o | w | n |
| d | a | r | k | b | s | s | l | m |
| h | r | e | p | s | t | d | j | p |

**Subtraction. Draw a line between the pairs that have the same answer.**

EXAMPLE:

a.  5 - 3 ———— 6 - 4
    3 - 3        9 - 1

b.  8 - 7        9 - 4
    3 - 1        5 - 3

c.  8 - 4        7 - 2
    7 - 5        5 - 1

d.  8 - 2        8 - 3
    9 - 5        7 - 3

e.  10 - 5       7 - 1
    12 - 6       9 - 4
    2 - 0        6 - 0

f.  5 - 5        14 - 7
    12 - 9       8 - 5
    11 - 4       8 - 8

> **John 3:36**
> "Whoever believes in the Son has eternal life, but whoever rejects the Son will not see life, for God's wrath remains on him."

**Day 13**

---

**Something is wrong with one word in each sentence. Find the word and correct it!**

1. i learned the Bible verse.

2. Gve him a brush.

3. You can sti on the chair.

4. Will you miks the paint?

5. Ded you get the pen?

# Day 13

**Circle the words that do not belong in the numbered lists below.**

EXAMPLE:

| | | | | | |
|---|---|---|---|---|---|
| 1. beans | carrots | corn | (balls) | peas | (books) |
| 2. train | boat | leg | car | dress | jet |
| 3. cat | orange | green | blue | red | five |
| 4. lake | ocean | pond | chair | river | shoe |
| 5. bear | apple | lion | wolf | pillow | tiger |
| 6. head | sleep | jump | hop | run | skip |
| 7. Jane | Kathy | Tom | Fred | Jill | Anne |
| 8. park | scared | happy | sad | mad | bee |
| 9. tulip | daffodil | wagon | daisy | basket | rose |
| 10. shirt | socks | bus | rope | pants | dress |

**Write a story that begins, "My favorite kind of fruit is _____ because…"**

_____
_____
_____
_____
_____
_____
_____
_____
_____
_____
_____
_____
_____

John 14:6
Jesus answered, "I am the way and the truth and the life. No one comes to the Father except through me."

**Day 14**

**Help Pocket and his friends find their doggy snacks by drawing a line to match each dog with the correct answer bone.**

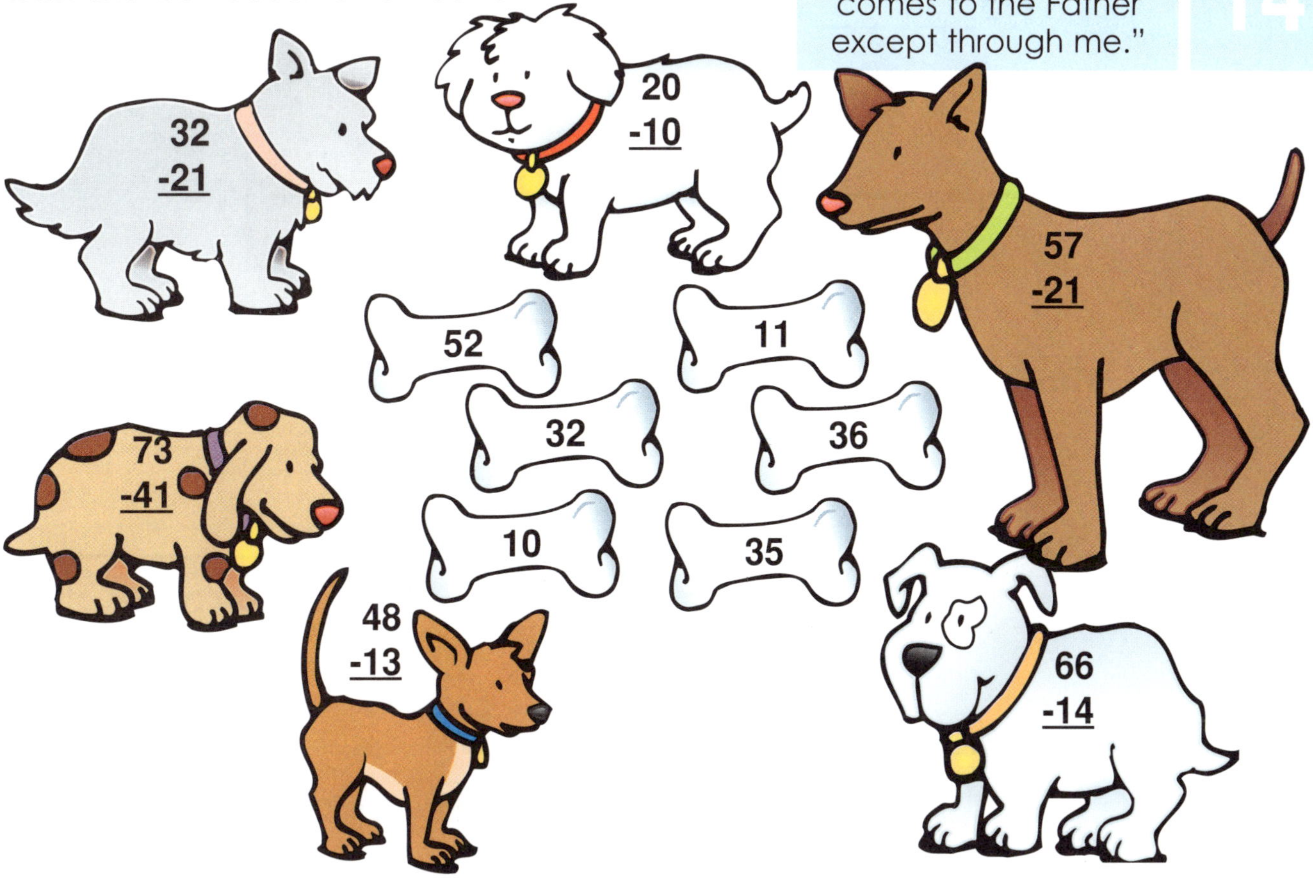


**Circle the letters that spell the ending sounds.**

| | | | | |
|---|---|---|---|---|
| EXAMPLE: math 12 -2 10 |  |  |  |  |
| (th) sh ch | th sh ch | th sh ch | th sh ch | th sh ch |
|  |  |  |  |  |
| th sh ch | th sh ch | th sh ch | th sh ch | th sh ch |

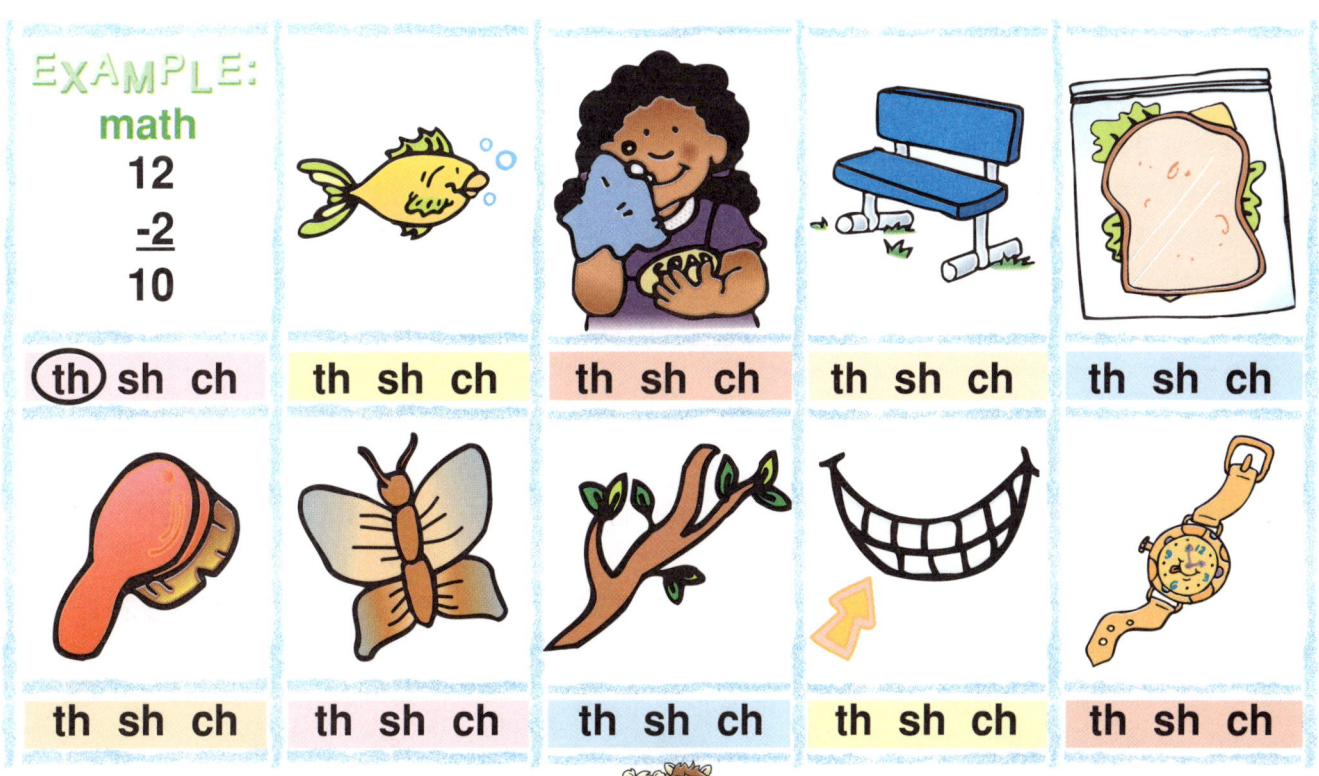

# Day 14

**Fill in the missing oi or oy; then write the word.**

b ___ ___
_____

s ___ ___ l
_____

___ ___ ster
_____

t ___ ___
_____

p ___ ___ nt
_____

---

**Write the correct word in the blank.**

1. Grayson _____ a hymn.          **sing**     **sang**
2. Did the bell _____ yet?           **ring**     **rang**
3. The bee _____ the king.         **stung**    **sting**
4. The waves will _____ the ship.    **sank**     **sink**
5. Mom will take a _____ trip.       **ship**     **short**
6. I _____ visit Grandma at home.    **shack**    **shall**
7. Lori has a _____ on her back.     **rash**     **rush**
8. Tanner likes to _____ in the puddles.   **last**   **splash**

**Finish the chart.**

**Thomas Carlyle:** To us also, through every star, through every blade of grass, is not God made visible if we will open our minds and our eyes.

# Day 15

1. 2, 4, 6, ___, ___, ___

2. 3, ___, 9, ___, ___, ___

3. 4, ___, 12, ___, ___, ___

4. 5, ___, 15, ___, ___, 30

**Use the Word Study List to do the following activity.**

**Word Study List**

go
me
we
he
no
so
she
be
see
bee

1. Write the word <u>go</u>. Change the beginning letter to make two more words.

2. Write the words that mean the opposite of <u>yes</u> and <u>stop</u>.

3. Write <u>she</u>; then write two more words that end the same.

# Day 15

Fill in the blank with a homonym for the underlined word.
**Remember**: Homonyms sound the same but have different meanings.

| made | new | ~~eight~~ | sea | through |
| wood | right | bee | hear | knot |

EXAMPLE:

1. Denise <u>ate</u> ____eight____ pancakes for breakfast.
2. Stay <u>here</u> and you can _____ the music.
3. Can you <u>see</u> the _____ from the top of the hill?
4. <u>Be</u> careful when you catch a _____.
5. <u>Would</u> you get some _____ for the fire?
6. Did you <u>write</u> the _____ answer?
7. He <u>threw</u> the ball _____ the window.
8. Our <u>maid</u> _____ all the beds.
9. The little girl could <u>not</u> tie a _____ in the rope.
10. My mother <u>knew</u> the _____ teacher.

**What did you do yesterday? Write down your activities in the order you did them.**

1. _____
2. _____
3. _____
4. _____
5. _____
6. _____

**Read and solve the math problem below.**

On July 4th, Rob and his friends went to the parade. It was a hot day. Rob bought five snow cones. He gave one to Grayson, one to Denise, and one to Allie. How many snow cones did Rob have left?

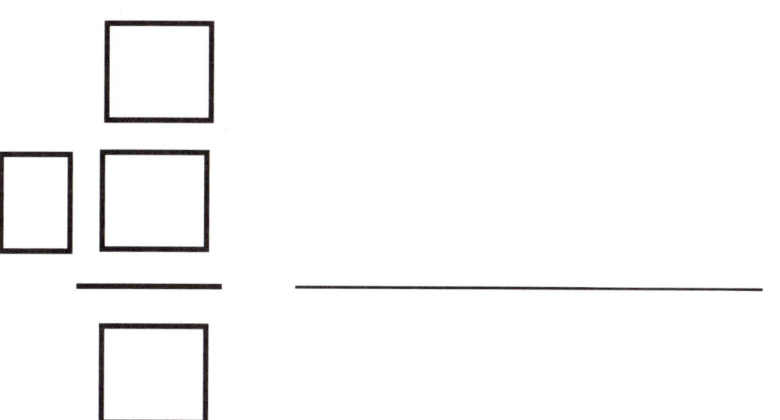

**Romans 5:8**
But God demonstrates his own love for us in this: While we were still sinners, Christ died for us.

**Day 16**

---

**Divide the following compound words.** EXAMPLE: snow/ball.

1. goldfish
2. blueberry
3. hairbrush
4. yourself
5. railroad
6. sometime
7. daytime
8. grapefruit
9. bedtime
10. popcorn
11. sailboat
12. today
13. spaceship
14. raindrop
15. newspaper
16. doghouse
17. cupcake
18. sidewalk

# Day 16

**Read and answer the questions.**

Years ago, many black-footed ferrets lived in the West. They were wild and free. Their habitat was in the flat grasslands. Their habitat was destroyed by man.

The ferrets began to vanish. Almost all of them died. Scientists worked to save the ferrets' lives, and now their numbers have increased.

1. Where did the black-footed ferrets live?
   _____

2. Who worked to save the ferrets' lives?
   _____

3. What happened when the scientists started to work?
   _____

**How many words can you make using the letters in "Ten Commandments"?**

tent

**Subtraction.**

> **Romans 8:28**
> And we know that in all things God works for the good of those who love him...

**Day 17**

| 10 | 10 | 10 | 10 | 10 | 10 | 10 | 10 | 10 |
|----|----|----|----|----|----|----|----|----|
| -2 | -9 | -7 | -1 | -8 | -3 | -4 | -6 | -5 |

| 11 | 11 | 11 | 11 | 11 | 11 | 11 | 11 | 11 |
|----|----|----|----|----|----|----|----|----|
| -2 | -9 | -7 | -1 | -8 | -3 | -5 | -0 | -6 |

| 12 | 12 | 12 | 12 | 12 | 12 | 12 | 12 | 12 |
|----|----|----|----|----|----|----|----|----|
| -2 | -9 | -7 | -1 | -8 | -3 | -5 | -0 | -6 |

**Write a story.**

If I were a firecracker, I would...

# Day 17

**Number the sentences in their correct order.**

_____ Lori's friend made a wish and blew out the candles.
_____ Lori put sixteen blue candles on the cake.
_____ Lori made a chocolate cake for her friend.
_____ Lori went to the store and bought a cake mix.
_____ Lori lit the candles with a match.

**Draw a picture of the birthday cake Lori made for her friend.**

**Match the sign shapes to the correct answer and then color the signs.**

   yield
         yellow

   hospital
         blue

   railroad crossing
         black/white

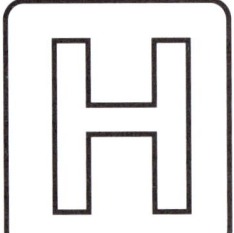   phone
         blue

   stop
         red

   handicapped
         blue

Which balloon has the number described by the tens and ones? Color that balloon. Use the color that is written in each box.

**Romans 10:17**
Consequently, faith comes from hearing the message, and the message is heard through the word of Christ.

**Day 18**

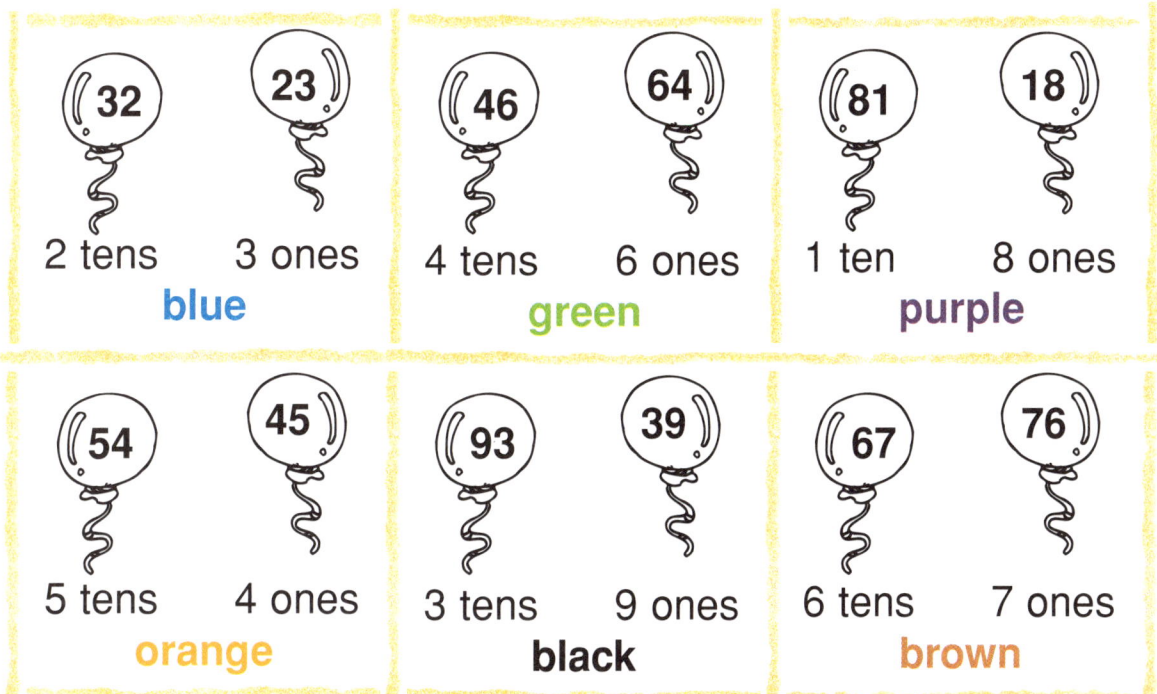

One word is spelled wrong in each sentence. Write the correct word from the word list.

**Word Study and Spelling List**

help
met
next
leg
pet
net
wet

1. A cat is a good pat.

2. She ran to get hlp.

3. He sat nekst to her.

4. We mit on the bus.

5. The dog cut his lag.

6. The duck got wit.

7. The fish is in the nut.

www.summerbrains.com © Summer Bridge Activities™ 1–2

# Day 18

**Read the sentences. Circle the nouns (naming words).**

EXAMPLE:
1. The (horse) lost one of his (shoes).
2. The dog ran after the mailman.
3. A submarine is a kind of boat.
4. The nurse read a book to the sick lady.
5. What kind of sandwich did you have in your lunch?
6. Our teacher showed us a movie about butterflies.
7. The artist drew a beautiful picture of the city.
8. My little sister has a cute teddy bear.
9. Does Mr. Fredrickson have the key for the back door?
10. The boys and girls left for Vacation Bible school.

---

**Write the months of the year in the correct order.**

| March | February | April | August |
| November | January | May | December |
| June | September | July | October |

1. _____
2. _____
3. _____
4. _____
5. _____
6. _____
7. _____
8. _____
9. _____
10. _____
11. _____
12. _____

1. Circle the odd numbers in each row.

**1 Corinthians 10:31**
So whether you eat or drink or whatever you do, do it all for the glory of God.

**Day 19**

a. 2   5   7   3   9   4   6   11
b. 1   10   6   8   12   13   15   2
c. 5   11   9   13   14   17   19   3

2. Circle the even numbers in each row.

a. 6   9   2   11   4   7   3   8
b. 13   8   10   6   12   16   9   5
c. 14   16   9   11   12   18   7   4

3. Circle the largest number in each set.

a. 26 or 32   c. 51 or 49   e. 41 or 14
b. 19 or 21   d. 80 or 60   f. 67 or 76

Write the middle consonant of each word below.

pea____ut   sho____el   Je____us   ti____er

flo____er   wi____dow   un____appy   va____uum

**Day**

Read each sentence. Write the correct word on the line.

1. A dime is a _____.
   coin   point   lawn

2. I want to buy my friend a new _____.
   boy   toy   claw

3. My cat has one white _____.
   paw   saw   car

4. Don has two sons and one _____.
   paw   daughter   boil

**Invent, design, and describe a new kind of soda pop!**

**Fill in the blank space with a number to get the answer in the box.**

> **1 Corinthians 13:4**
> Love is patient, love is kind. It does not envy, it does not boast, it is not proud.

**Day 20**

4 - ___ = **3**
3 + ___ = 
2 + ___ = 

5 + ___ = **6**
2 + ___ = 
9 - ___ = 

7 + ___ = **8**
___ - 1 = 
___ + 2 = 

___ - 4 = **5**
8 - ___ = 
3 + ___ = 

**Fill in each blank with the correct contraction.**

EXAMPLE:
1. cannot    can't
2. I am    _____
3. you are    _____
4. do not    _____
5. he is    _____
6. I will    _____
7. you have    _____

**Write the two words that make up the contraction.**

8. isn't    _____
9. you've    _____
10. she's    _____
11. couldn't    _____
12. we're    _____
13. didn't    _____
14. they'll    _____

**Day 20**

Fill in the blanks using <u>is</u> or <u>are</u>. On line 9, write a sentence using <u>is</u>. On line 10, write a sentence using <u>are</u>.

1. We _____ going to town tomorrow.
2. The cows _____ in the field.
3. This book _____ not mine.
4. Where _____ a box of chalk?
5. Seals _____ fast swimmers.
6. _____ he going to help you?
7. It _____ very hot outside today.
8. _____ you going to the circus?
9. _____
10. _____

Read the sentences. Put a (.), (!), or (?) at the end of each one.

1. What time do you go to bed___
2. Why did the baby cry___
3. That girl over there is my sister___
4. We do not have our work done___
5. Get out of the way___
6. Are you and I going to the movie___
7. Go shut the door___
8. Did you enjoy the sermon___
9. My parents are going on a long trip___
10. Look out___ That car will run over you___

# Words to Sound, Read, and Spell

## Magic e

| | |
|---|---|
| can | cane |
| mad | made |
| cap | cape |
| man | mane |
| tap | tape |
| past | paste |
| bit | bite |
| kit | kite |
| quit | quite |
| win | wine |
| rip | ripe |
| hid | hide |
| grip | gripe |
| slid | slide |

## Long a (ā) words to know!

| | | | |
|---|---|---|---|
| bake | brake | cave | rake |
| pale | shape | wake | blaze |
| state | chase | tape | rate |
| shade | brave | waste | plane |
| name | plate | wave | taste |
| make | made | flake | gave |
| scale | game | drape | snake |
| late | lake | vase | scrape |
| mane | whale | came | base |
| frame | date | cake | shave |
| shake | cane | sale | awake |
| cape | blame | skate | grape |
| paste | take | trade | |
| save | glaze | same | |

## Long i (ī) words

| | | | |
|---|---|---|---|
| dive | pride | pipe | hide |
| bite | wipe | while | chime |
| time | spike | slide | tribe |
| tire | pie | like | shine |
| line | tie | die | smile |
| live | dime | glide | wide |
| quite | hire | gripe | trike |
| crime | hive | size | alike |
| wife | white | prize | stripe |
| pine | slime | mine | strike |
| pile | life | five | lie |
| side | nine | kite | inside |
| hike | mile | lime | swipe |
| alive | ride | wire | |
| ripe | bike | fine | |
| file | bribe | drive | |

## Long o (ō) words

| | | | |
|---|---|---|---|
| rope | wore | hose | home |
| more | rose | those | |
| slope | chore | toe | |
| store | stole | code | |
| pose | smoke | tone | |
| quote | bone | drove | |
| doze | wove | throne | |
| rode | zone | pole | |
| stone | stove | mole | |
| dove | cone | joke | |
| shone | poke | shore | |
| hole | froze | note | |
| chose | hope | those | |
| hoe | sore | sole | |
| tore | nose | swore | |
| scope | score | woke | |

## ŌK, I know I can do it!

| | | |
|---|---|---|
| bow | slow | mellow |
| low | elbow | blow |
| mow | fellow | |
| grow | yellow | |
| snow | willow | |
| show | pillow | |
| throw | hollow | |
| bowl | flow | |
| own | tomorrow | |
| grown | rainbow | |
| thrown | snowman | |
| flown | window | |
| blown | widow | |

## These words say ō, too!

| |
|---|
| no |
| so |
| go |
| hello |
| Jell-O |
| Eskimo |
| hippo |
| lingo |
| jumbo |
| lasso |
| banjo |
| condo |

## ow and ou

### ow

| | | |
|---|---|---|
| cow | crowd | growl |
| down | power | prowl |
| town | shower | chow |
| gown | towel | brow |
| clown | now | allow |
| crown | how | powder |
| drown | plow | drowsy |
| frown | owl | chowder |
| brown | howl | |

### ou

| | | |
|---|---|---|
| out | found | mouse |
| shout | round | sour |
| about | sound | flour |
| trout | pound | ground |
| scout | count | account |
| loud | mount | thousand |
| cloud | around | discount |
| aloud | surround | county |
| bound | house | |

## oi words

| | |
|---|---|
| oil | join |
| boil | joint |
| coil | point |
| soil | appoint |
| broil | disappoint |
| spoil | poison |
| void | |
| coin | |

www.summerbrains.com     © Summer Bridge Activities™ 1–2

| *au* words | *oy* words | *aw* words | *ai* says ā | | |
|---|---|---|---|---|---|
| haul | boy | dawn | pain | rain | quail |
| fault | toy | fawn | main | saint | grain |
| vault | joy | drawn | paint | maid | faith |
| fraud | enjoy | claw | paid | pail | strain |
| cause | joyful | straw | jail | brain | snail |
| haunt | loyal | lawyer | stain | wait | |
| haunted | royal | hawk | bait | afraid | |
| launch | cowboy | crawl | braid | nail | |
| gauze | tomboy | shawl | sail | plain | |
| because | corduroy | awful | train | laid | |
| | convoy | seesaw | trail | tail | |
| | employ | outlaw | aid | chain | |
| | soybean | | mail | faint | |
| | | | fail | raid | |

### Two *e*'s are better than one!

| | | | | | |
|---|---|---|---|---|---|
| see | keep | cheese | nineteen | beep | squeeze |
| deep | geese | meet | tree | street | need |
| seem | beet | fifteen | sneeze | creep | peel |
| sweet | three | Jeep | peek | sheep | wheel |
| weep | breeze | sleet | feed | screech | |
| sheet | seek | sleep | cheek | bleed | |
| sweep | seed | reef | weed | deed | |
| speech | feel | seen | teen | bee | |
| green | tweed | steel | screen | peep | |
| queen | speed | beef | sixteen | freeze | |
| teeth | greed | feet | wee | free | |

### Soft *c*: ce, ci, cy

| | | |
|---|---|---|
| cent | mice | office |
| celery | spice | fancy |
| center | race | mercy |
| cereal | fence | spicy |
| cement | nice | lacy |
| celebrate | circus | officer |
| ice | circle | medicine |
| dance | pencil | face |
| once | excited | place |
| twice | decide | |
| slice | exciting | |
| space | recipe | |

### *ea* says ē

| | | | | |
|---|---|---|---|---|
| sea | beast | cream | peak | clean |
| leave | seat | eat | lead | feast |
| meal | leader | reach | leap | neat |
| dream | leak | bean | deal | beaver |
| flea | bead | east | team | beak |
| peach | treat | meat | pea | read |
| real | reason | beach | weave | cheat |
| scream | seam | lean | steal | season |
| heat | tea | yeast | steam | weak |
| preach | heave | wheat | beat | grease |
| mean | seal | teacher | teach | |

Summer Bridge Activities™ *for Young Christians*

# Motivational Calendar!

Month _____

My parents and I decided that if I complete 15 days of *Summer Bridge Activities™ for Young Christians* and read ____ minutes a day, my incentive/reward will be:

_____

Child's Signature _____ Parent's Signature _____

Day 1  ☆ 🕊 📖 ____          Day 9  ☆ 🕊 📖 ____

Day 2  ☆ 🕊 📖 ____          Day 10 ☆ 🕊 📖 ____

Day 3  ☆ 🕊 📖 ____          Day 11 ☆ 🕊 📖 ____

Day 4  ☆ 🕊 📖 ____          Day 12 ☆ 🕊 📖 ____

Day 5  ☆ 🕊 📖 ____          Day 13 ☆ 🕊 📖 ____

Day 6  ☆ 🕊 📖 ____          Day 14 ☆ 🕊 📖 ____

Day 7  ☆ 🕊 📖 ____          Day 15 ☆ 🕊 📖 ____

Day 8  ☆ 🕊 📖 ____

**Child:** Color the ☆ for daily activities completed.
Color the 🕊 for daily devotionals completed.
Color the 📖 for daily reading completed.
**Parent:** Initial the ____ when your child is complete.

**Fun Activity Ideas to Go Along with the Third Section!**

1. Play hopscotch, marbles, or jump rope.
2. Visit a fire station.
3. Take a walk around your neighborhood. Name all of the trees and flowers you can.
4. Make up a song.
5. Make a hut out of blankets and chairs.
6. Put a note in a helium balloon and let it go.
7. Start a journal. Write about your favorite vacation memories.
8. Make 3-D nature art. Glue leaves, twigs, dirt, grass, and rocks on paper.
9. Find an ant colony. Spill some food and see what happens.
10. Play charades.
11. Make up a story by drawing pictures.
12. Do something to help the environment. Clean up an area near your house.
13. Weed a row in the garden. Mom will love it!
14. Take a trip to a park.
15. Learn about different road signs.

**Subtraction.**

1 Corinthians 13:8
Love never fails.

**Day 1**

A.   15    14    16    17    13
     - 4   - 2   - 8   - 3   - 4

B.   10    18    13    11    16
     - 4   - 7   - 6   - 9   - 5

C.   17    12    10    18    19
     - 8   - 5   - 1   - 4   - 9

**Synonyms** are words that have the same or nearly the same meaning. Find a synonym in the train for each of the words below. Write the word on the line.

begin _____   afraid _____   trace _____

sick _____   shut _____   fast _____

glad _____   simple _____   silly _____

large _____   big _____   neat _____

# Day 1

Unscramble the scrambled word in each sentence and write it correctly.

1. A <u>brzea</u> is an animal in the zoo. _____
2. The robin has <u>nowlf</u> away. _____
3. We mixed flour and eggs in a <u>owlb</u>. _____
4. Button your button and zip your <u>rpzipe</u>. _____
5. A lot of <u>leppeo</u> were at the game. _____
6. We met our new teacher <u>yatdo</u>. _____
7. My old <u>oessh</u> do not fit my feet. _____
8. We made a list of <u>ngtihs</u> to get. _____
9. Jim got <u>irtyd</u> when he fell in the mud. _____
10. <u>eSktri</u> three and you're out. _____

Draw a new invention and label each of its parts and uses:

**Addition.**

**Henry Ward Beecher:** It's easier to go down a hill than up it but the view is much better at the top.

# Day 2

```
  3    6    9    5    4    2    3    5
  5    4    2    1    3    3    3    5
 +2   +3   +2   +2   +4   +5   +4   +3
 ──   ──   ──   ──   ──   ──   ──   ──

  4    7    1    6    2    8    4    3
  5    2    8    1    3    2    2    7
 +3   +1   +1   +4   +2   +3   +6   +1
 ──   ──   ──   ──   ──   ──   ──   ──
```

7 + 3 + 1 = _____       8 + 2 + 2 = _____       3 + 5 + 1 = _____

---

Read the sentences. Find a synonym for each underlined word. Write the new word on the lines. A synonym is a word that has the same or nearly the same meaning as another.

| automobile | small | glad | rush |

The baby is very <u>tiny</u>.
_____
_____

The <u>car</u> ran out of gas.
_____
_____

Susan won, so she was very <u>happy</u>.
_____
_____

My mother was in a big <u>hurry</u>.
_____
_____

# Day 2

Make an X by the answers to the questions.

## How is a snake like a turtle?

____ 1. They both have shells.
____ 2. They both can be found on land.
____ 3. They are both reptiles.
____ 4. They both fly in the sky.
____ 5. They both have tails.
____ 6. They both eat flies.
____ 7. They both have legs.

## How is a bike like a truck?

____ 1. They both have tires.
____ 2. They both need gas.
____ 3. They both can be different colors.
____ 4. They can both be new and shiny.
____ 5. They both have four wheels.
____ 6. They both can go.
____ 7. You can ride in both of them.

## How is a sailor like a doctor?

____ 1. They both wear white.
____ 2. They both wear hats.
____ 3. They both work with dogs.
____ 4. They both are people.
____ 5. Their job is to help sick people.
____ 6. They have to work on a ship.
____ 7. They both should be helpful.

**Finish the story.**

One day Denise went out to play. Her friend, Lori, was already outside. Lori said to Denise, "Let's go play…"

_____
_____
_____
_____
_____

© Summer Bridge Activities™ 1–2         www.summerbrains.com

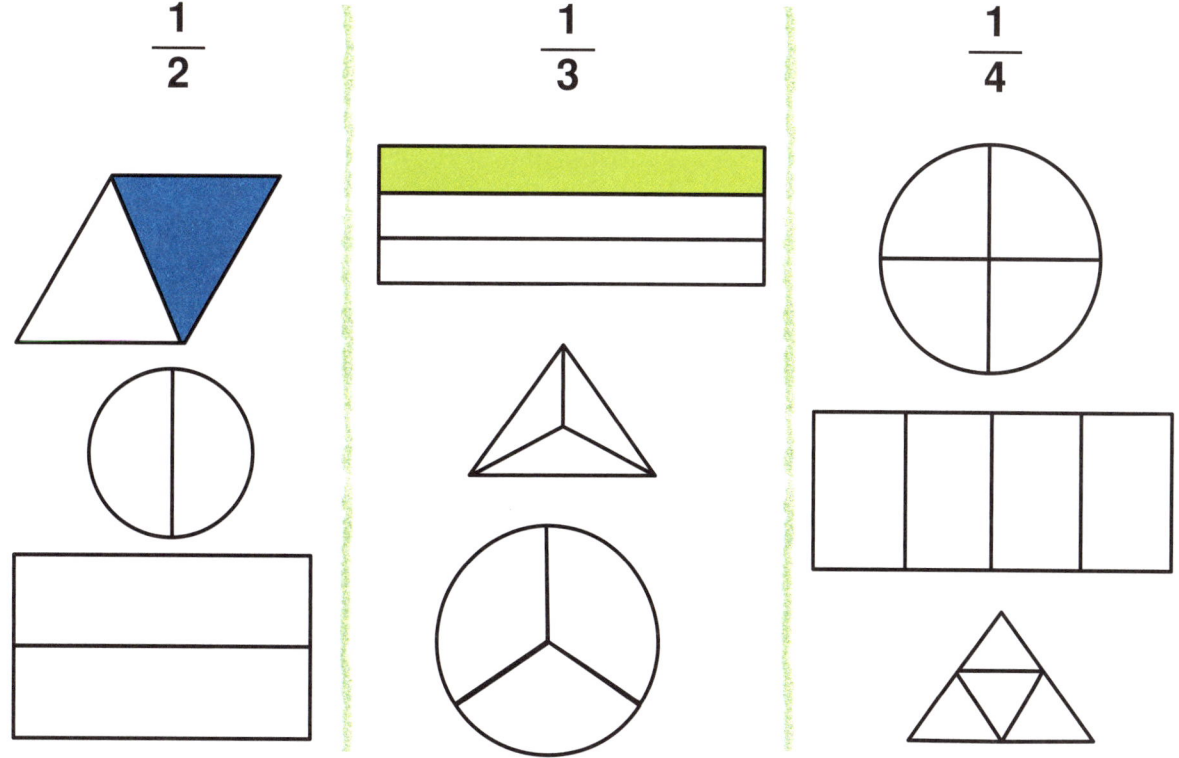

**2 Corinthians 5:17**
Therefore, if anyone is in Christ, he is a new creation; the old has gone, the new has come!

**Day 3**

**Color in the correct fraction of each picture.**

EXAMPLE:

$\frac{1}{2}$ $\frac{1}{3}$ $\frac{1}{4}$

**Color the matching bat and ball with the same color.**

EXAMPLE:

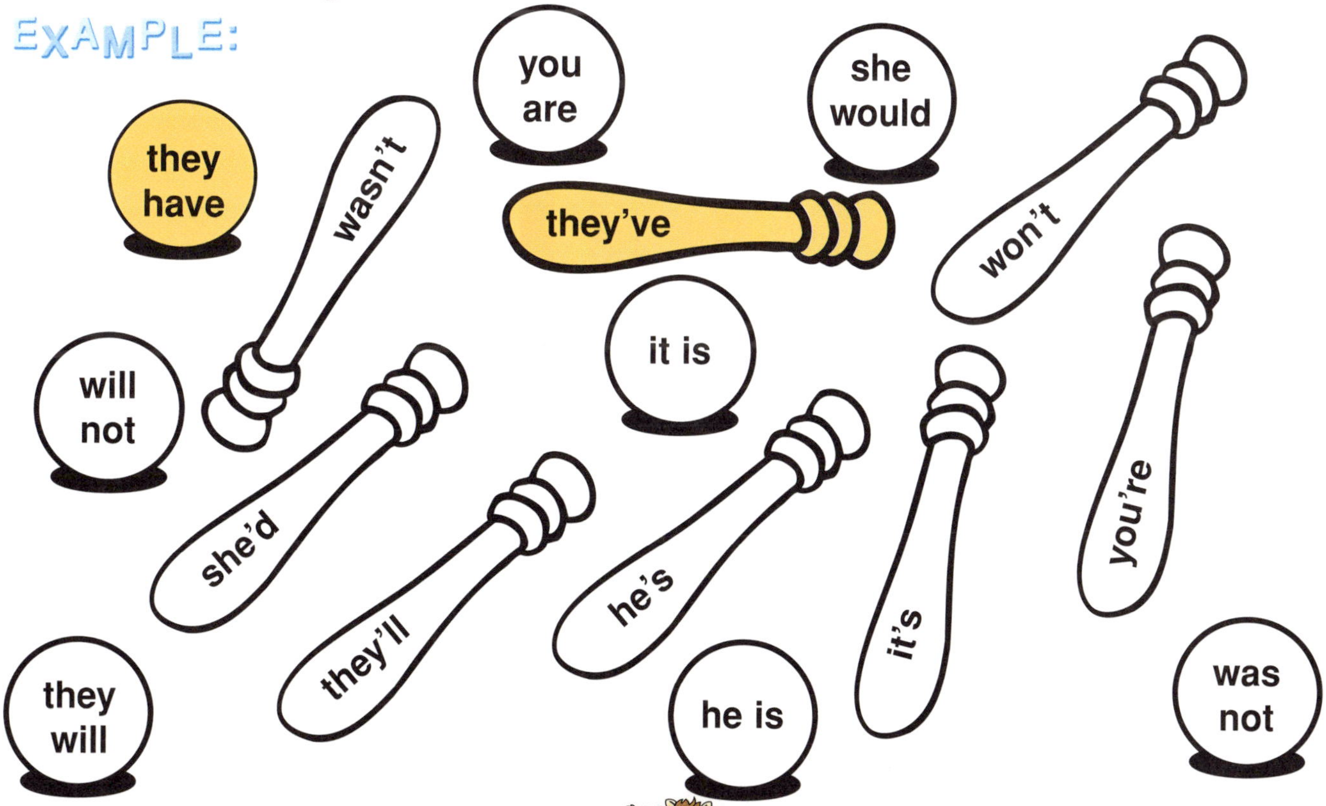

they have
they've
you are
she would
wasn't
won't
will not
it is
she'd
they'll
he's
it's
you're
they will
he is
was not

# Day 3

Make up five funny sentences using one word from each column on the hot-air balloon. Do not use any of the words more than once.

children   held
robbers    fed
bugs       followed
bears      found
birds      dropped

1. _____ the balloons.

2. _____ a big truck.

3. _____ the silly cow.

4. _____ the green frog.

5. _____ all the people.

Read the words in the right column. Write the words in alphabetical order in the left column. Draw your favorite animal in the box.

1. _____ pig
2. _____ horse
3. _____ cat
4. _____ frog
5. _____ ant
6. _____ bear
7. _____ giraffe
8. _____ deer
9. _____ elephant
10. _____ monkey

**Add or subtract.**

**Galatians 6:7**
A man reaps what he sows.

**Day 4**

| 11 | 18 | 3 | 10 | 17 | 13 | 18 | 19 |
|----|----|---|----|----|----|----|----|
| +7 | +1 | +7 | -3 | -2 | +6 | -6 | -7 |

| 33 | 64 | 5 | 2 | 12 | 14 | 27 | 16 |
|----|----|---|---|----|----|----|----|
| +5 | -3 | +3 | +4 | -7 | -11 | -3 | -8 |

17 + 2 = _____    11 - 3 = _____    13 + 5 = _____

---

**Unscramble the words.**

psto _____     ithkn _____

sfat _____     rypa _____

ltpae _____    ppayh _____

pste _____     seay _____

gbrni _____    dbyo _____

itfha _____    stfri _____

enwt _____    yrc _____

**Day**

Read the words aloud; then write them in alphabetical order.

1. _____   6. _____

rabbit
snake
lion
dog
fish
dish
make
candy
puppy
vase

2. _____   7. _____

3. _____   8. _____

4. _____   9. _____

5. _____   10. _____

**Dairy Designs.** A dairy company has asked you to create a design for a milk carton. Create and color an original milk carton design for the company.

Color the coins that match the given amount.

**Claude M. Bristol:** It's the constant and determined effort that breaks down all resistance and sweeps away all obstacles.

# Day 5

Match the homonyms. **Homonyms** are words that sound the same but have different meanings.

EXAMPLE:

| ate | heel | flower | through |
| cent | sea | threw | pair |
| knight | night | pain | hear |
| our | one | pear | flour |
| write | right | know | pane |
| knew | sent | here | male |
| heal | eight | maid | blew |
| see | hare | mail | no |
| hair | new | sail | made |
| won | hour | blue | sale |

www.summerbrains.com © Summer Bridge Activities™ 1–2

**Day**  Read these silly sentences! Put a  by your favorite sentence.

1. You can spend a day at the beach without money.

2. A yardstick has three feet, but it really cannot walk.

3. You might whip cream, but it will not cry.

4. It is not mean to beat scrambled eggs.

5. Rain falls sometimes, but it never gets hurt.

6. You do not eat a whole lot if you eat the hole of a donut.

**Draw four things that belong in each box.**

**Things in the ocean**

**Things in the sky**

**Things in a cave**

**Add or subtract.**

> **Ephesians 4:32**
> Be kind and compassionate to one another, forgiving each other, just as in Christ God forgave you.

**Day 6**

1.  10   18    7    7    8    6    9    4    9
    -4   -14  -3   +5   +2   -4   -4   +7   +2

2.  11   11   10    9    8    9    7   10   11
    -1   +8   -8   +8   +2   +1   -5   -3   -7

8 + 6 = _____     9 + 3 = _____     4 + 9 = _____

**Antonyms. Match the words with opposite meanings.**

EXAMPLE:
strong — weak
young, sad, bad, over, old, good, happy, under

add, inside, wet, float, always / never, sink, outside, subtract, dry

light, fat, tall, on, slow / thin, off, fast, dark, short

**Day**

Read each sentence. Do what it tells you to do. Then put a ✓ in the box to show that you have finished that step.

**Let's get ready for lunch.**

☐ Draw a plate on the place mat.
☐ Draw a napkin on the left side of the plate.
☐ Draw a fork on the napkin.
☐ Draw a knife and spoon on the right side of the plate.
☐ Draw a glass of purple juice above the napkin.
☐ Draw your favorite lunch.

**Enjoy!**

**Writing.**

If I could fly anywhere, I would fly to _____ because... _____

_____
_____
_____
_____
_____
_____
_____
_____

Finish each table.

**Ephesians 6:1**
Children, obey your parents in the Lord, for this is right.

# Day 7

| Add 10 | |
|---|---|
| EXAMPLE: 5 | 15 |
| 8 | |
| 7 | |
| 9 | |
| 3 | |
| 4 | |

| Add 8 | |
|---|---|
| 2 | |
| 6 | |
| 4 | |
| 7 | |
| 3 | |
| 5 | |

| Add 6 | |
|---|---|
| 10 | |
| 6 | |
| 8 | |
| 7 | |
| 4 | |
| 5 | |

Circle the correctly spelled word in each row.

1. ca'nt     can'nt     can't
2. esy     easy     eazy
3. crie     cri     cry
4. kea     key     kee
5. buy     buye     biy
6. lihg     light     ligte
7. allready     already     alredy
8. summ     som     some
9. sekond     secund     second
10. hasn't     has'nt     hasent
11. wonce     onse     once
12. pritty     preety     pretty
13. carry     carey     carrie
14. you're     yure     yo're
15. parte     part     parrt
16. star     stor     starr
17. funy     funny     funnie
18. babie     babey     baby
19. mabe     maybe     maybee
20. therde     therd     third

# Day 7

**Circle the correct answer.**

1. Another name for boy is:    girl    son    funny
2. After seven comes:    six    nine    eight
3. I bite with:    wheel    teeth    arms
4. A car and truck roll on:    with    whip    wheels
5. A farmer grows:    ship    wheat    land
6. Your brain helps you:    this    thing    think
7. A chair can also be a:    seat    sound    safe
8. A rabbit has:    while    whirl    whiskers

**Do the crossword puzzle.**

**Word List**

cent

sent

here

night

write

weight

**Down**

1. A penny is worth one _____.
2. My friend _____ me a letter.
3. Please _____ your name.

**Across**

1. Will you please come _____?
2. When the sun goes down, it is _____.
3. The doctor checked my _____.

Make number sentences. Remember: Use only the numbers in the circles.

**Philippians 2:5**
Your attitude should be the same as that of Christ Jesus.

# Day 8

EXAMPLE:

( 13  8  5 )

( 12  5  7 )

8 + 5 = 13
___ + ___ = ___
___ - ___ = ___
___ - ___ = ___

___ + ___ = ___
___ + ___ = ___
___ - ___ = ___
___ - ___ = ___

( 14  8  6 )

( 6  9  15 )

___ + ___ = ___
___ + ___ = ___
___ - ___ = ___
___ - ___ = ___

___ + ___ = ___
___ + ___ = ___
___ - ___ = ___
___ - ___ = ___

**Word List**

| | |
|---|---|
| bone | fox |
| those | coat |
| log | rock |
| drove | top |
| job | rope |
| note | dock |

Put the words under the correct sound-picture.

long o (ō) nose   short o (ŏ)  pop

1.              1.
2.              2.
3.              3.
4.              4.
5.              5.
6.              6.

**Day 8**

Read the sentences. Circle and write the action verb in each sentence.

EXAMPLE:

1. The chicken (ran) away. __ran__
2. Judy cut her finger with the knife. _____
3. A kangaroo can hop very fast. _____
4. I like to read the Psalms. _____
5. Ted and Sid will chop some wood. _____
6. That kitten likes to climb trees. _____
7. We will eat dinner at six o'clock. _____
8. The baby was yawning. _____
9. The plate crashed to the ground. _____
10. Please peel this orange for me. _____

**Draw a face beside each statement that tells how it makes you feel.**

1. a rainy day

2. chocolate cake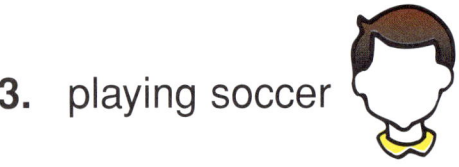

3. playing soccer

4. camping in the mountains

5. fighting with a friend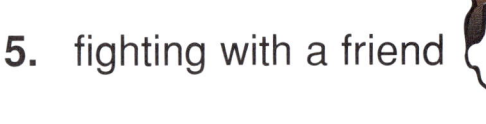

6. taking a bath

7. birthday presents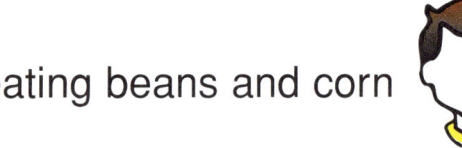

8. eating beans and corn

9. catching a fly ball

10. going to Grandmother's

**Add.**

**Philippians 4:13**
I can do everything through him who gives me strength.

# Day 9

1.     3     3     6     2     4     5     7     3
         2     4     1     2     3     4     1     5
       +1    +2    +2    +3    +3    +6    +2    +4

2.     1     6     7     4     5     4     8     4
         3     3     2     5     2     4     1     6
       +2    +1    +1    +2    +3    +1    +2    +3

Write soft <u>c</u> words under <u>pencil</u>. Write hard <u>c</u> words under <u>candy</u>.

| grocery | cattle | cement | corn | price |
|---------|--------|--------|------|-------|
| cake    | cellar | crib   | grace | cow  |

pencil       candy

1. _____     1. _____

2. _____     2. _____

3. _____     3. _____

4. _____     4. _____

5. _____     5. _____

**Day** Unscramble the sentences. Write the words in the correct order.

1. sun shine will today The.

2. mile today I a walked.

3. house We painted our.

4. Mother knit will I something for.

**Write a letter. Ask a friend to attend church with you.**

Start your letter with "Dear _____,"
End your letter with "Yours truly, _____."

Color the shape that matches the description.

**Vincent Lombardi:** Leaders aren't born, they are made. And they are made just like anything else, through hard work.

# Day 10

2 tens     3 ones

*green*

5 tens     7 ones

*purple*

5 tens     2 ones

*yellow*

2 tens     3 ones

*orange*

3 tens     9 ones

*red*

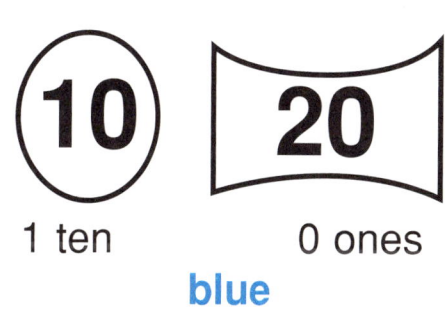

1 ten     0 ones

*blue*

---

Write each word under the correct sound-picture.

| tower | blow | mow | clown | elbow | crown |
| flown | bowls | how | frown | own | brown |

**cow**           **pillow**

**Day** Draw a line to the right word.

EXAMPLE:

1. Something near you is — — — — — — — — clock
2. Something that tells time is a — — — — — bird
3. A time of day is — — — — — — — — — — — babies
4. A crow is a kind of — — — — — — — — — snoop
5. A place where fish live is an — — — — — close
6. Tuna is a kind of                                   dusk
7. Chicks, ducklings, and fawns are kinds of   aquarium
8. A shop is a kind of                              strike
9. To hit something is to                         store
10. To look in someone else's things is to    fish

**Write as many words as you can that describe…**

  ice cream

  watermelon

**Subtract.**

> **1 Timothy 2:5**
> For there is one God and one mediator between God and men, the man Christ Jesus.

**Day 11**

| 57 | 68 | 96 | 57 | 38 | 59 | 64 | 77 | 54 |
|---|---|---|---|---|---|---|---|---|
| -32 | -44 | -92 | -43 | -3 | -45 | -42 | -34 | -20 |

| 83 | 75 | 48 | 95 | 68 | 39 | 89 | 93 | 69 |
|---|---|---|---|---|---|---|---|---|
| -62 | -20 | -4 | -31 | -26 | -10 | -53 | -10 | -35 |

| 19 | 24 | 52 | 63 | 76 | 88 | 90 | 71 | 29 |
|---|---|---|---|---|---|---|---|---|
| -3 | -11 | -31 | -41 | -22 | -44 | -30 | -51 | -15 |

---

**Write in the name of each picture and color.**

so ___      gr ___ s      ___ sh

sh ___ t      ___ ove      gat ___

**Day**

Read each sentence. Do what it tells you to do. Then put a ✔ in the box to show that you have finished that step.

**Let's go to the park and play.**

☐ Draw a swingset.
☐ Draw a slide.
☐ Draw a sandpile.
☐ Draw green grass.
☐ Draw one apple tree.
☐ Draw a yellow sun in the sky.
☐ Draw a blue sky.

**Have fun!**

Before school starts again, I want to…

Finish each table.

**EXAMPLE:**

| subtract 5 | |
|---|---|
| 9 | 4 |
| 5 | |
| 7 | |
| 10 | |
| 11 | |
| 8 | |

| subtract 3 | |
|---|---|
| 10 | |
| 9 | |
| 7 | |
| 8 | |
| 6 | |
| 11 | |

| subtract 2 | |
|---|---|
| 11 | |
| 7 | |
| 9 | |
| 5 | |
| 8 | |
| 6 | |

2 Timothy 2:15
Do your best to present yourself to God as one approved.

# Day 12

Circle the correct r-controlled vowel.

**EXAMPLE:** b(ir)d

# Day 12

**Complete the riddles.**

1. I am rather tiny. I have wings and buzz around. I can be a real pest at picnics. I am a _____.

2. I was just born. My mother and father feed me and keep me dry. I cry and sleep, but I cannot walk. I am a _____.

3. I am made of metal and am quite little. I can lock things up and open them, too! I am a _____.

4. I like to sing. I lay eggs. I like to eat bugs and worms. I am a _____.

**Retell the story of Noah's Ark.**

_____
_____
_____
_____
_____
_____
_____
_____
_____
_____

**Dale Carnegie:** Most ... important things ... have been accomplished by people who have kept on trying when there seemed to be no hope at all.

# Day 13

Math. Below are two mileage maps. Use them to answer the questions.

How many miles from Salt Lake City to Bountiful? _____ miles

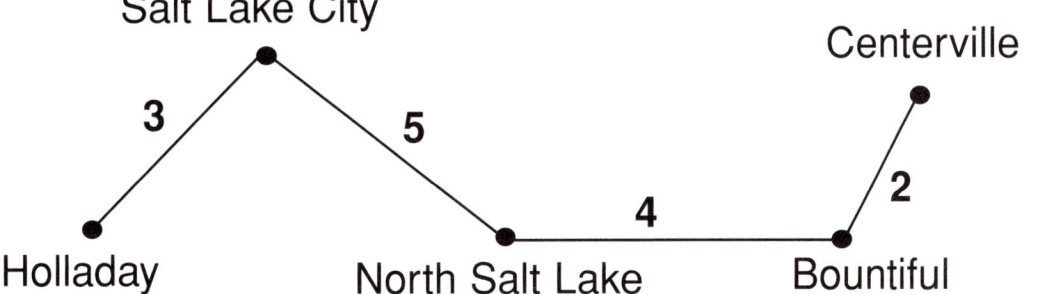

How many miles from Provo to Pleasant Grove? _____ miles

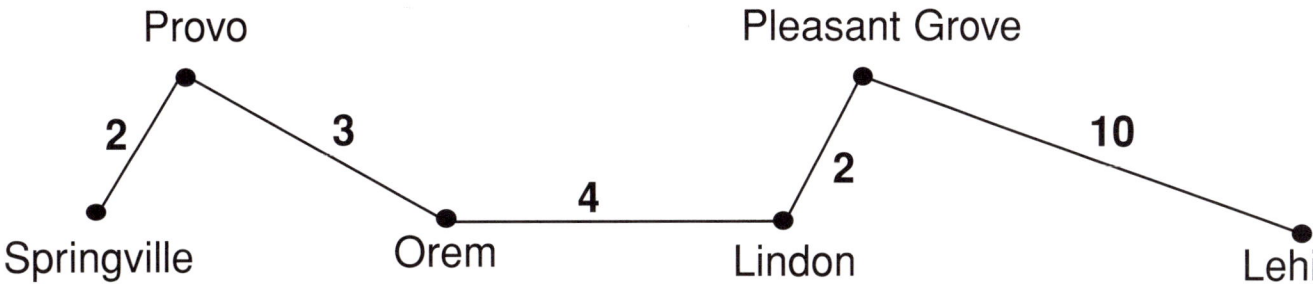

Read the sentences. Is the underlined word in each sentence spelled right or wrong? Circle the correct answer.

EXAMPLE: Jane is a very <u>brav</u> girl.   right   (wrong)

1. 
2. The American flag is red, white, and <u>bloo</u>.   right   wrong
3. Those girls are in my <u>class</u>.   right   wrong
4. Mike is a very <u>helpfull</u> friend.   right   wrong
5. I remembered to turn off the <u>light</u>.   right   wrong
6. This candy is sticky <u>stuf</u>.   right   wrong
7. Is <u>shee</u> coming with us?   right   wrong
8. May I <u>yooz</u> your book?   right   wrong
9. Don't <u>lose</u> your boots.   right   wrong
10. Our baby is so <u>cute</u>.   right   wrong

# Day 13

Noisy or quiet? Put an <u>N</u> in front of things that are noisy and a <u>Q</u> in front of things that are quiet. Draw a noisy picture and a quiet picture.

**Noisy**

____ 1. A butterfly flying through the air.

____ 2. A cook using a mixer to make a cake.

____ 3. Popcorn popping on the stove.

____ 4. A dress hanging up to dry.

____ 5. A child reading to herself.

____ 6. Ice cream melting in the sun.

____ 7. A cat and dog fighting in the driveway.

____ 8. A band marching in a parade.

**Quiet**

---

**Homonyms.** The following words sound and are spelled the same but have two different meanings. Write two sentences using the different meanings.

**bat:**     a wooden stick that is used to hit a ball
           a small animal that flies at night

_____
_____
_____
_____

**spring:**   the season of the year between winter and summer
              to jump or bounce into the air

_____
_____
_____
_____

**Hebrews 13:8**
Jesus Christ is the same yesterday and today and forever.

# Day 14

Add or subtract.

1.  24    16    28    37    42    12    20    28
   +12    − 0   −14   −26   +27   +11   +25   −11

2.  87¢   79¢    3    15¢    97    40    25    66
   −16¢  −54¢  +13   +24¢   −64   +40   −25   +33

3.  12    18    41    66    13    30    64   124
    40    20     6    22    22    12    25   112
   +62   +11   +32   +11   +24   +10   +10  +203

---

Circle either g or j below each word to show which sound the g makes.

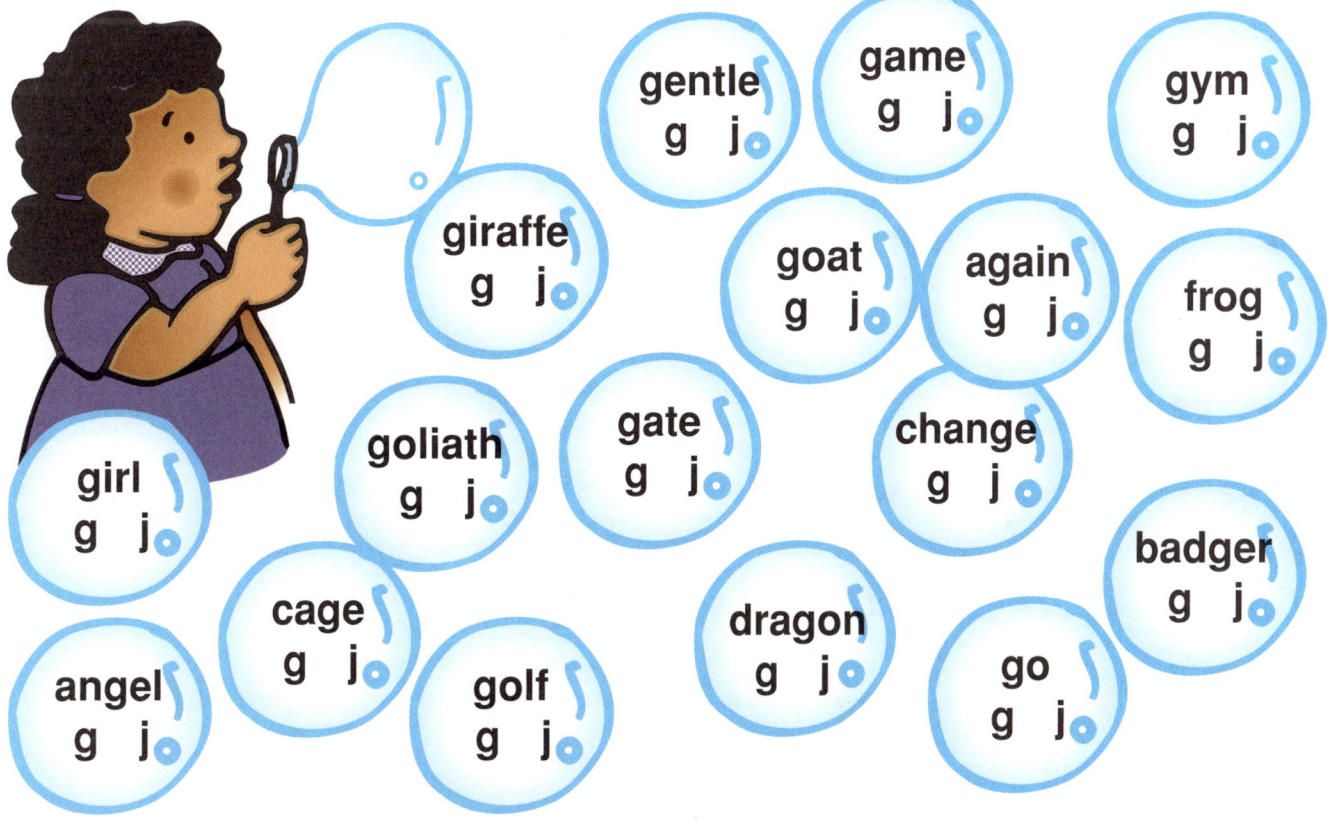

gentle  game  gym
g j    g j   g j

giraffe  goat  again  frog
g j     g j   g j    g j

girl  goliath  gate  change  badger
g j   g j     g j   g j     g j

angel  cage  golf  dragon  go
g j   g j   g j   g j     g j

# Day 14

Answer the riddles. Write the correct short a (ă) word on the line. Then draw a picture of your answer in the box.

The mother of baby kittens is a ___ ___ ___.

To play baseball you need a ball and ___ ___ ___.

When we cross the street, hold my ___ ___ ___ ___.

**Match the words that rhyme.**

EXAMPLE:

goat — tree        shoe      hair
last    band       chair     two
bee  — boat        mean      rain
sand    fast       train     bean

Write the number of gumballs in each picture.

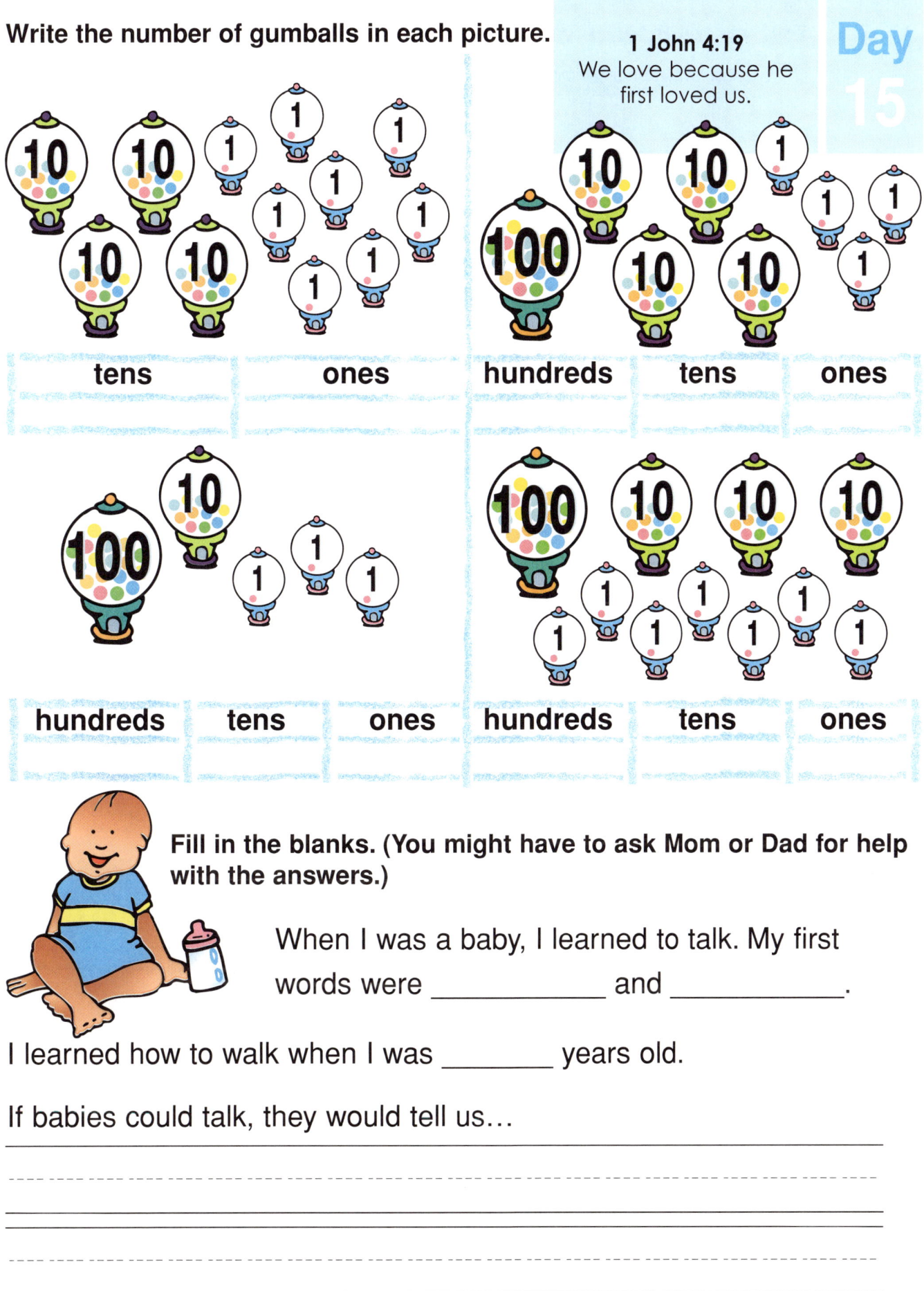

1 John 4:19
We love because he first loved us.

Day 15

Fill in the blanks. (You might have to ask Mom or Dad for help with the answers.)

When I was a baby, I learned to talk. My first words were _____ and _____.

I learned how to walk when I was _____ years old.

If babies could talk, they would tell us…
_____
_____
_____
_____

# Day 15

End each sentence with the correct mark. Use a (.), (!), or (?).

Allie went to the zoo ____
The tigers scared Allie ____
Do you like the zoo ____

Rob said a prayer ____
Pigs are huge and messy ____
What is your favorite animal ____

Write a sentence or two.

"I can be safe this summer by…" (For example: staying away from rivers, not getting sunburned, keeping my bike out of the road when I ride, etc.)

# Words to Sound, Read, and Spell

## ar / or / er / ir / ur

| ar | | | or | | | er | ir | ur |
|---|---|---|---|---|---|---|---|---|
| car | harm | chart | for | born | dorm | her | dirt | hurt |
| far | charm | party | fort | corn | form | clerk | shirt | spurt |
| jar | barn | bark | sort | worn | torch | perch | first | burnt |
| star | yarn | dark | short | thorn | porch | nerve | third | burp |
| scar | art | mark | sport | north | order | verb | swirl | curl |
| yard | dart | park | cork | forth | organ | fern | skirt | turtle |
| card | cart | shark | fork | forty | story | were | firm | purple |
| hard | part | spark | pork | horse | history | serve | bird | church |
| arm | smart | | stork | storm | | | thirst | |
| farm | start | | | | | | twirl | |

## Remember these special sounds!

### sh
| | |
|---|---|
| shed | brush |
| shell | slash |
| ship | flash |
| shack | clash |
| shag | trash |
| shin | crash |
| shock | smash |
| shot | fish |
| shop | dish |
| shuck | fresh |
| wish | |
| hush | |
| mush | |
| rush | |

### ch
| | |
|---|---|
| check | inch |
| chess | pinch |
| chick | chug |
| chill | chap |
| chin | chaff |
| chip | |
| chop | |
| chum | |
| chat | |
| much | |
| such | |
| rich | |
| which | |

### th / tch
| th | tch |
|---|---|
| this | hatch |
| them | patch |
| that | stitch |
| thud | scotch |
| math | catch |
| with | ditch |
| moth | |
| thin | **wh** |
| then | when |
| thick | where |
| bath | whip |
| path | why |
| cloth | what |
| path | |

## Compound words surprise us!

| | |
|---|---|
| pancake | rosebud |
| cupcake | bluebird |
| handshake | blueberry |
| cannot | frostbite |
| sunset | potpie |
| suntan | necktie |
| sandbox | wishbone |
| swingset | fireman |
| pineapple | nickname |
| sunrise | drumstick |
| sunshine | checkup |
| underline | |
| tiptoe | |
| bathrobe | |

## Here are -nt, -nd, -nk, and -ng words.

### -nt
| | |
|---|---|
| ant | spent |
| pant | mint |
| plant | hint |
| bent | print |
| dent | flint |
| rent | hunt |
| sent | stunt |
| tent | punt |
| vent | runt |
| went | |

### -nd
| | |
|---|---|
| and | blond |
| band | end |
| hand | bend |
| sand | send |
| land | lend |
| stand | tend |
| grand | spend |
| bond | wind |
| pond | fund |

### -nk
| | |
|---|---|
| bank | wink |
| yank | blink |
| sank | drink |
| tank | stink |
| drank | think |
| crank | honk |
| spank | bunk |
| ink | junk |
| pink | drunk |
| sink | skunk |

### -ng
| | |
|---|---|
| bang | long |
| rang | strong |
| hang | king |
| hung | sing |
| sung | wing |
| stung | bring |
| flung | swing |
| swung | thing |
| gong | |

## What about -y at the end of words?

| | |
|---|---|
| any | penny |
| many | puppy |
| very | sloppy |
| messy | happy |
| sticky | cherry |
| windy | angry |
| sandy | hungry |
| handy | sixty |
| copy | fifty |
| body | day |
| daddy | say |
| muddy | clay |
| candy | sway |
| twenty | may |
| dizzy | way |
| yummy | stay |
| funny | away |
| sunny | |

## These, too, are interesting!

| | | | |
|---|---|---|---|
| key | donkey | monkey | turkey |
| keys | donkeys | monkeys | turkeys |

### These are interesting words!

| | | |
|---|---|---|
| be | fume | dude |
| me | amuse | duke |
| he | abuse | tune |
| we | accuse | tube |
| she | value | few |
| eve | rescue | new |
| theme | continue | grew |
| extreme | blue | knew |
| complete | true | threw |
| compete | clue | crew |
| athlete | glue | drew |
| these | flute | news |
| cue | fluke | jewel |
| cute | rude | blew |
| cube | rule | flew |
| mule | prune | nephew |
| mute | due | stew |
| fuse | dune | |

### Here are some more -y words!

| | |
|---|---|
| cry | flying |
| why | crying |
| shy | trying |
| fry | typing |
| try | rhyming |
| by | hockey |
| fly | jockey |
| my | alley |
| sky | valley |
| spy | nosy |
| bye | trolley |
| lye | money |
| type | chimney |
| style | honey |
| rhyme | parsley |

### What about these?

| | |
|---|---|
| fly | flies |
| try | tries |
| | tried |
| cry | cries |
| | cried |
| fry | fries |
| | fried |

### Let's add the -s and -es sound.

| | | |
|---|---|---|
| flags | boxes | stitches |
| plants | foxes | crutches |
| hands | axes | matches |
| pets | sixes | benches |
| steps | buzzes | inches |
| belts | quizzes | patches |
| kids | buses | hatches |
| gifts | glasses | catches |
| bricks | kisses | pitches |
| dogs | dresses | stitches |
| socks | classes | blotches |
| songs | wishes | sketches |
| bugs | brushes | switches |
| trucks | dishes | |
| ducks | branches | |

### These words end with -ing.

| | | |
|---|---|---|
| jumping | coasting | whizzing |
| planting | peeking | winning |
| thinking | feeling | shopping |
| yelling | screaming | hugging |
| singing | reaching | tugging |
| catching | sailing | running |
| fishing | reading | swimming |
| quacking | making | hitting |
| poking | hoping | hopping |
| shaking | shining | sitting |
| riding | hiding | stopping |
| waving | skating | digging |
| smiling | diving | petting |
| joking | saving | grinning |
| floating | sledding | wagging |

### Add -ed and what do you get?

| | | |
|---|---|---|
| added | tested | grinned |
| ended | dumped | hugged |
| handed | crossed | dragged |
| mended | tripped | fanned |
| hinted | dropped | hummed |
| acted | snapped | tugged |
| dented | hopped | joked |
| dusted | camped | hiked |
| carted | missed | smiled |
| started | dripped | stared |
| rented | stopped | waved |
| petted | passed | cared |
| nodded | pumped | choked |
| rested | farmed | shaped |
| drifted | harmed | |

### Let's go for the -le endings.

| | | |
|---|---|---|
| paddle | raffle | crumble |
| saddle | sniffle | dimple |
| middle | apple | simple |
| riddle | bubble | handle |
| puddle | gobble | candle |
| cuddle | dribble | tackle |
| battle | nibble | crackle |
| rattle | pebble | freckle |
| kettle | wiggle | pickle |
| settle | jiggle | tickle |
| little | giggle | twinkle |
| bottle | juggle | sprinkle |
| dazzle | snuggle | buckle |
| sizzle | scramble | chuckle |
| puzzle | mumble | uncle |
| ruffle | tumble | tangle |
| shuffle | stumble | dangle |

### Let's read contractions!

| are | have | is, has | will | would, had |
|---|---|---|---|---|
| you're | I've | he's | I'll | I'd |
| we're | you've | it's | she'll | she'd |
| they're | we've | she's | he'll | you'd |
| who're | they've | what's | it'll | who'd |
| | could've | that's | we'll | he'd |
| **us** | should've | who's | they'll | they'd |
| let's | would've | there's | that'll | |
| | | here's | who'll | |
| **am** | | one's | you'll | |
| I'm | | | | |

### How about these endings?

| | | |
|---|---|---|
| bigger | helper | children |
| biggest | camper | chicken |
| fatter | winner | ladder |
| fattest | runner | matter |
| fresher | swimmer | better |
| freshest | singer | dresser |
| sicker | happen | pepper |
| sickest | fasten | slipper |
| longer | often | zipper |
| longest | rotten | dinner |
| pitcher | gotten | robber |
| catcher | bitten | offer |
| kicker | kitten | butter |
| hunter | kitchen | bumper |

# Answer Pages

# Section 1

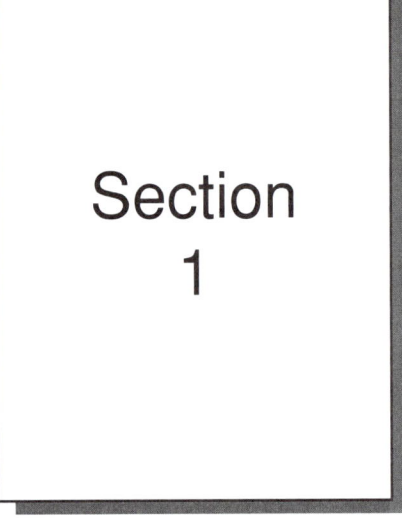
Page 3

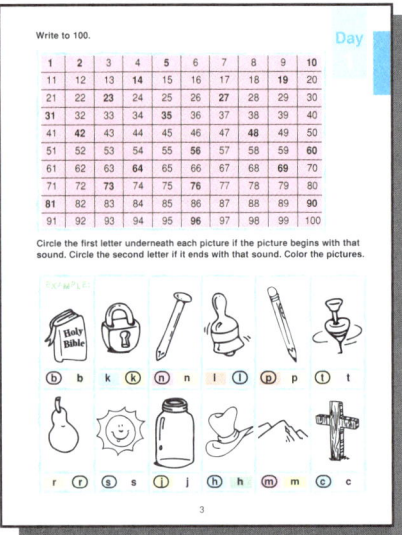
Page 4

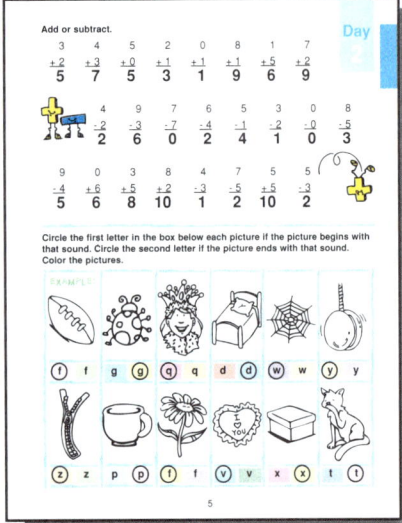
Page 5

Page 6

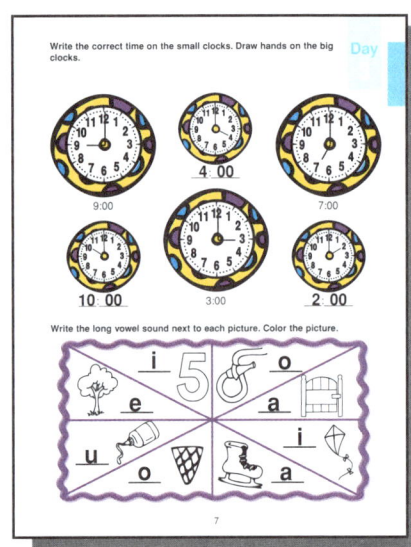
Page 7

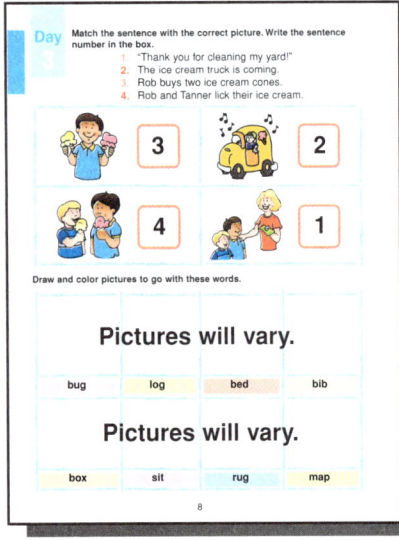
Page 8

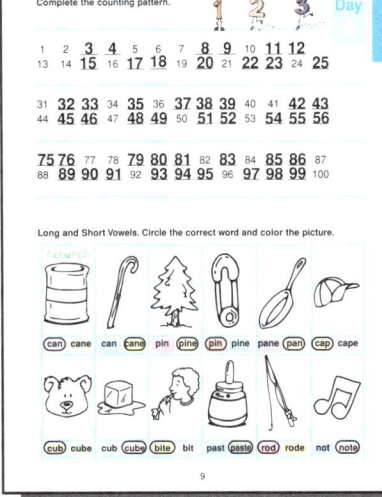
Page 9

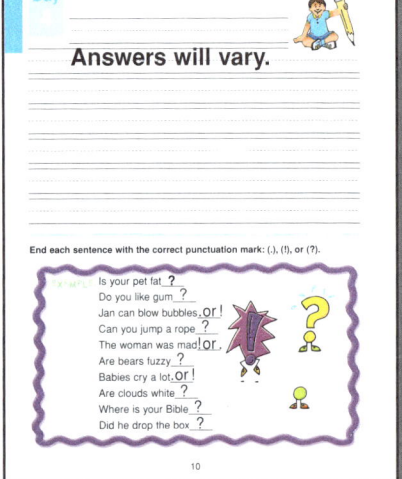
Page 10

Page 11

Page 12

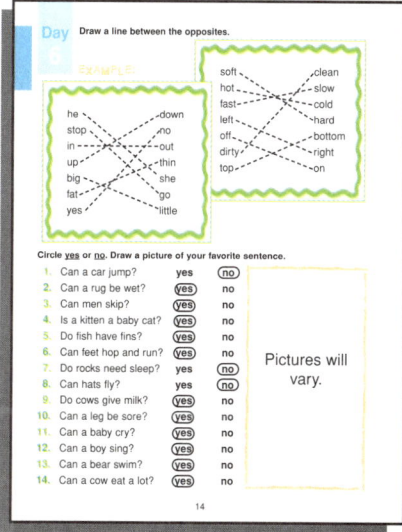
Page 13

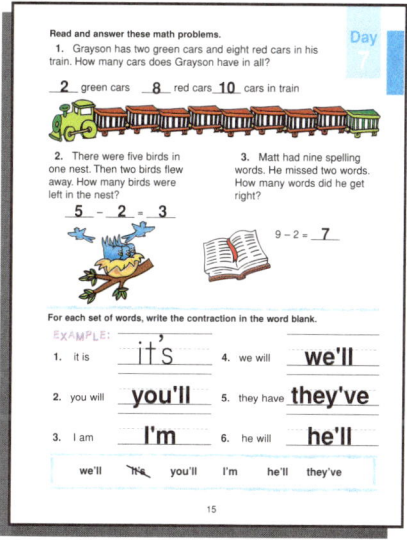
Page 14

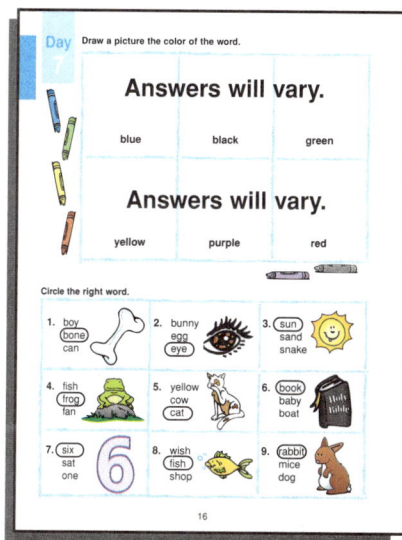
Page 15

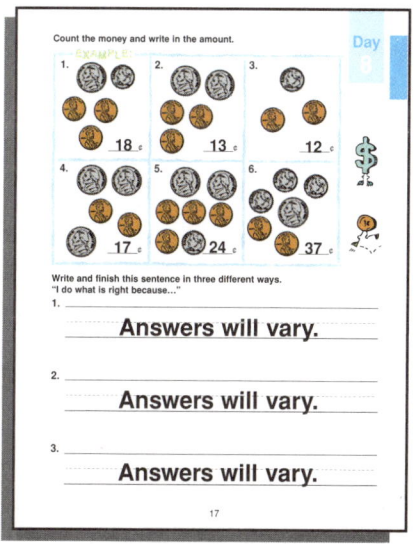
Page 16

Page 17

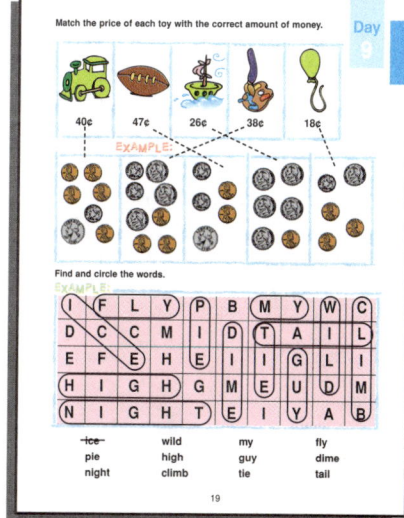
Page 18

Page 19

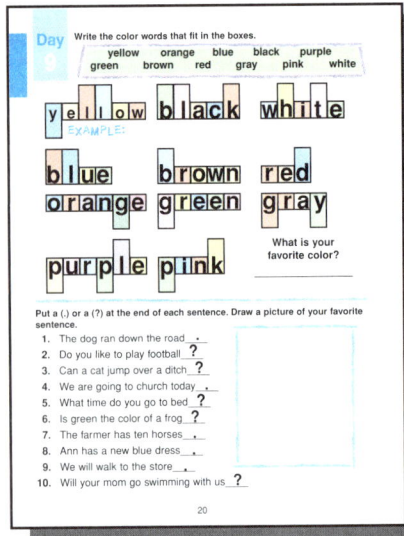 Page 20

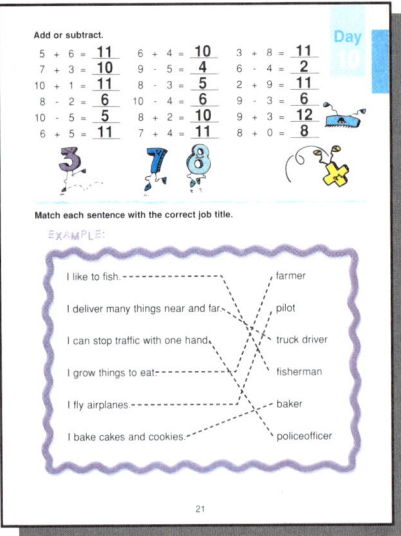 Page 21

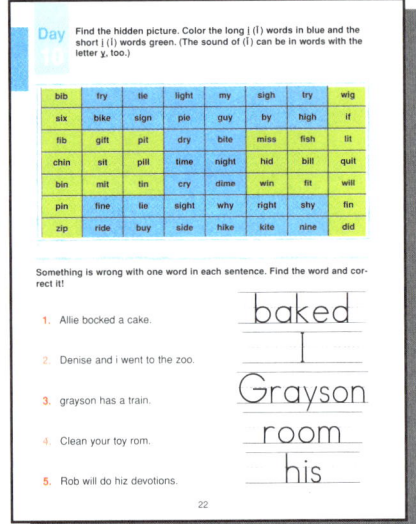 Page 22

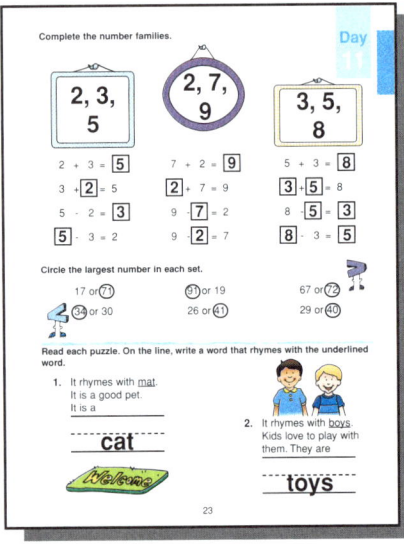 Page 23

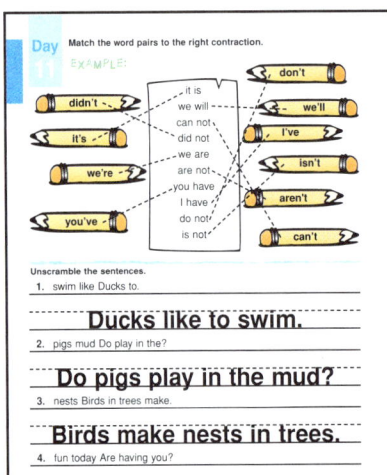 Page 24

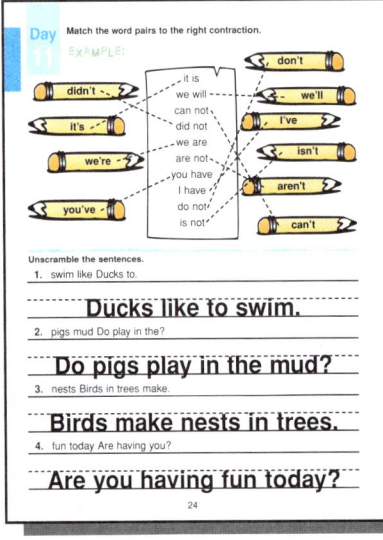 Page 25

 Page 26

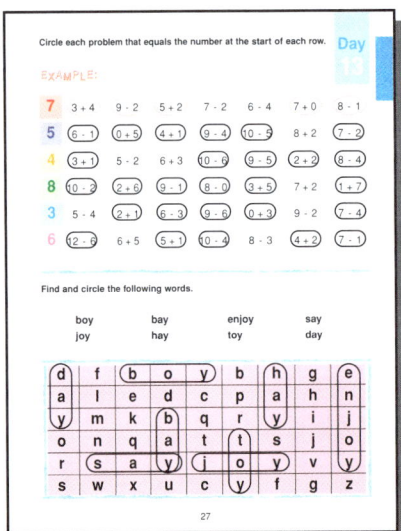 Page 27

Page 29

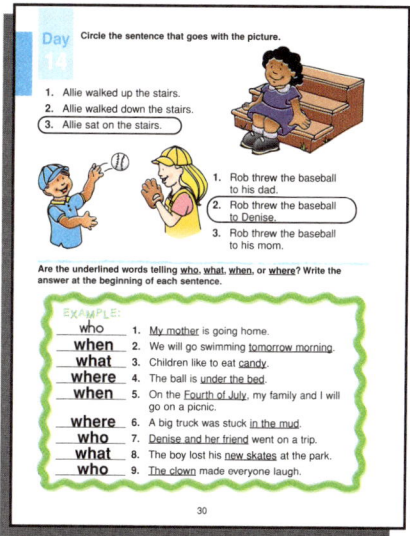
Page 30

Page 31

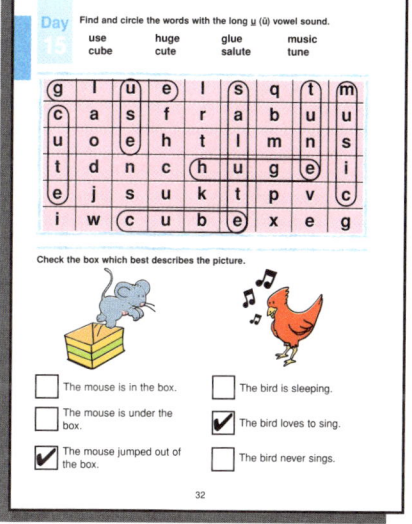
Page 32

Section 2

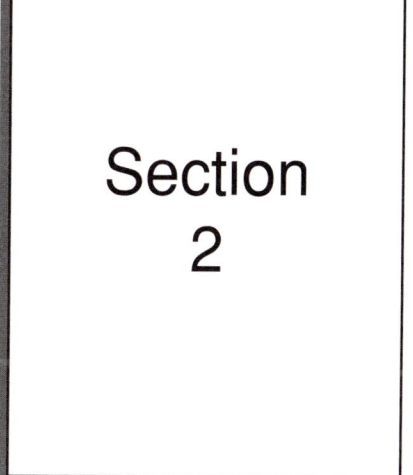
Page 37

Page 38

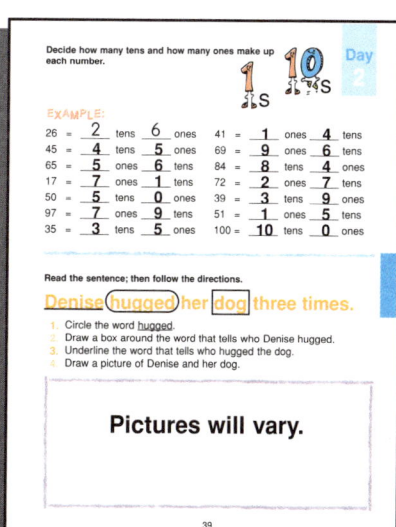
Page 39

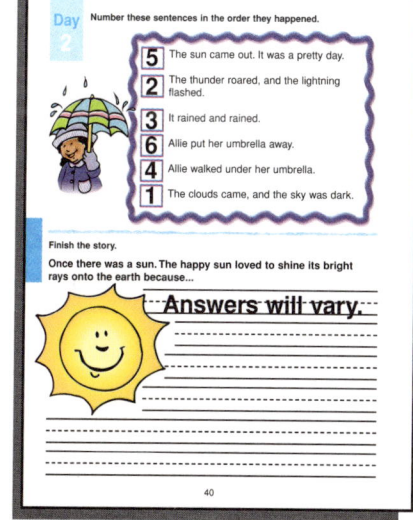
Page 40

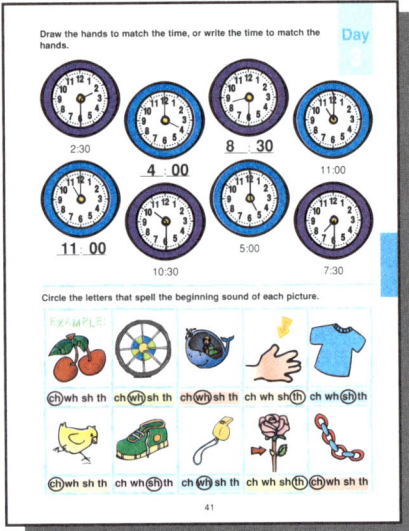
Page 41

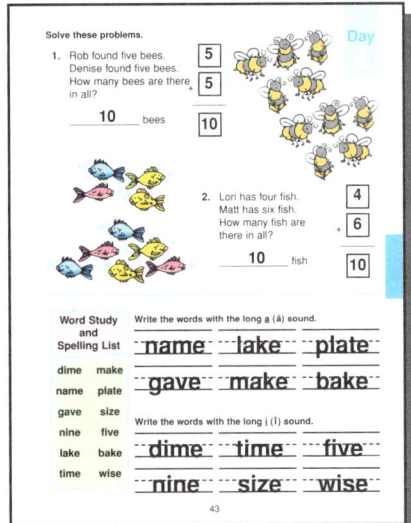
Page 42

Page 43

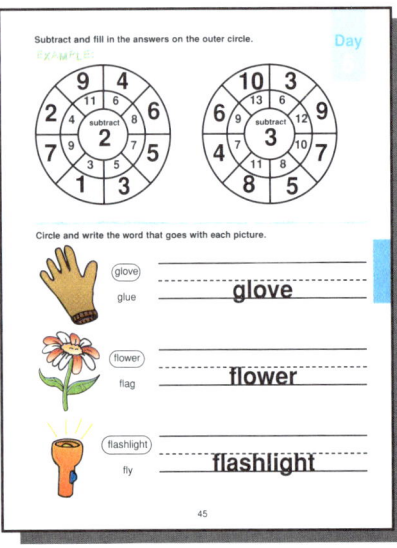
Page 44

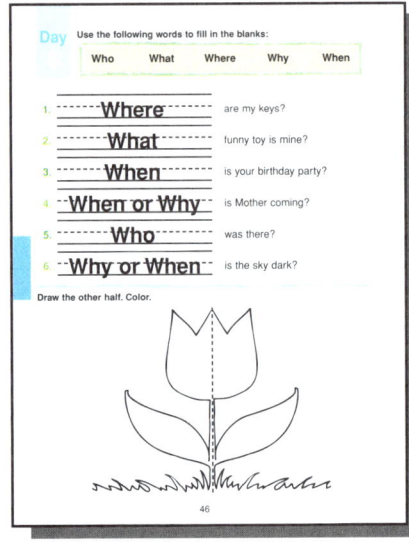
Page 45

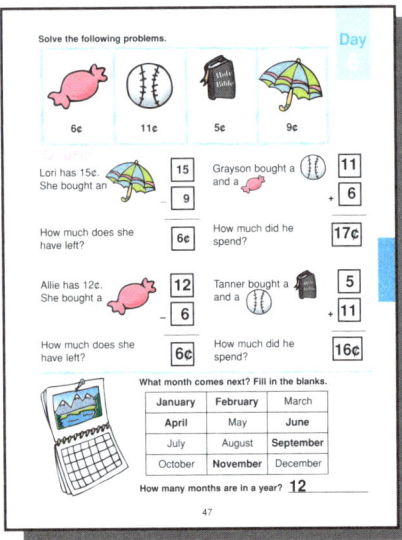
Page 46

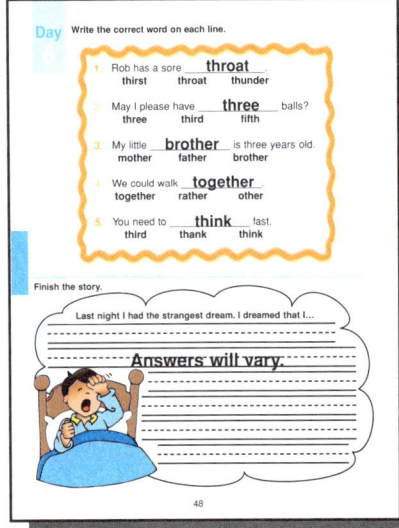
Page 47

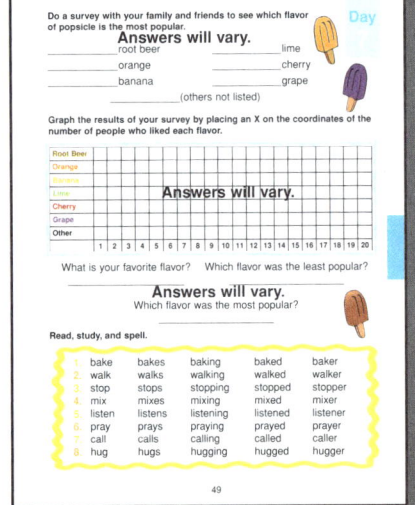
Page 48

Page 49

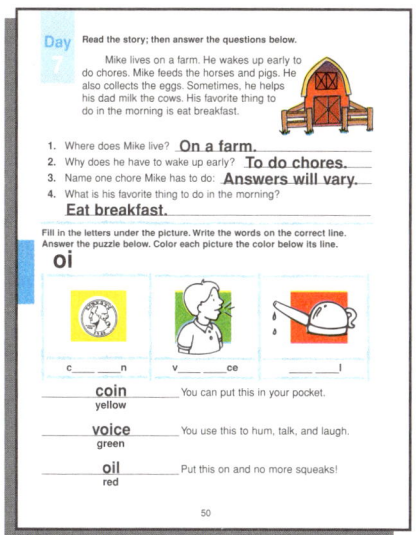
Page 50

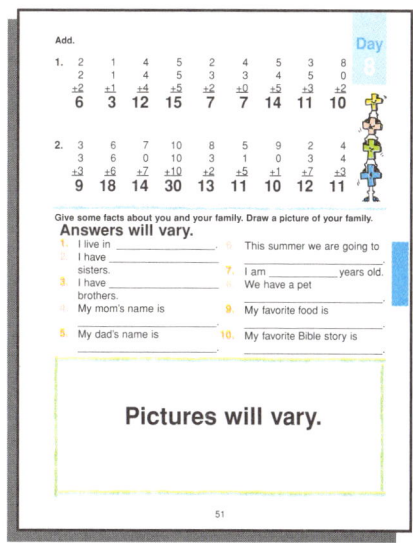
Page 51

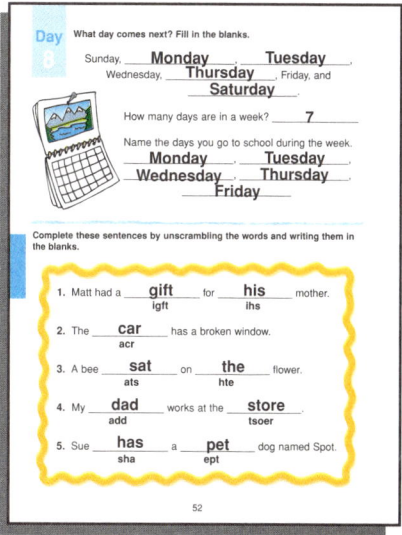
Page 52

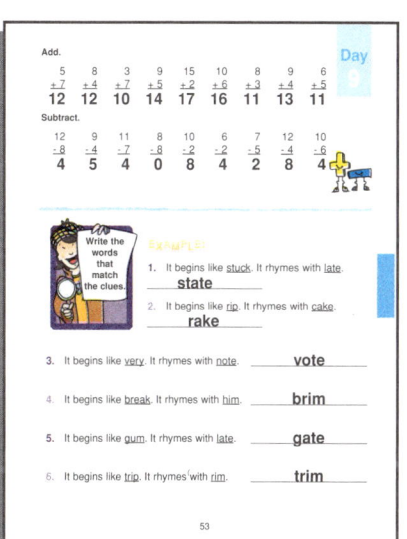
Page 53

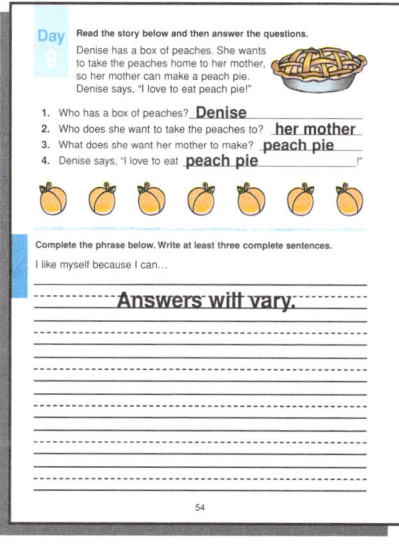
Page 54

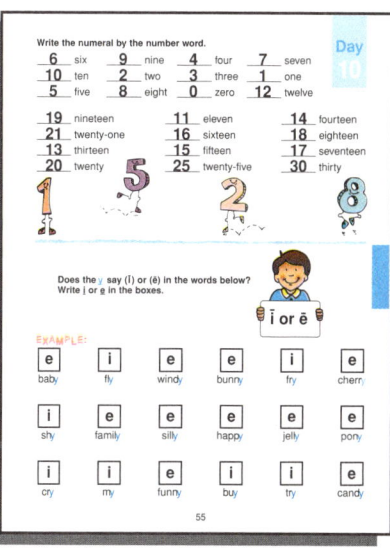
Page 55

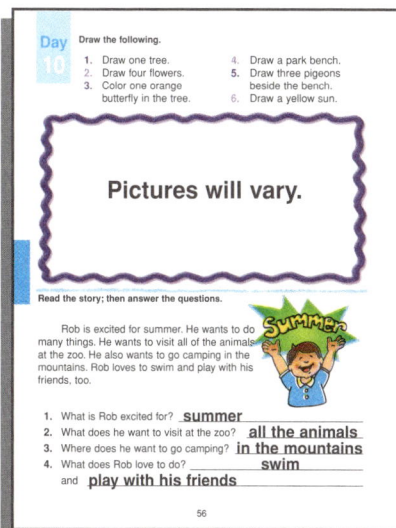
Page 56

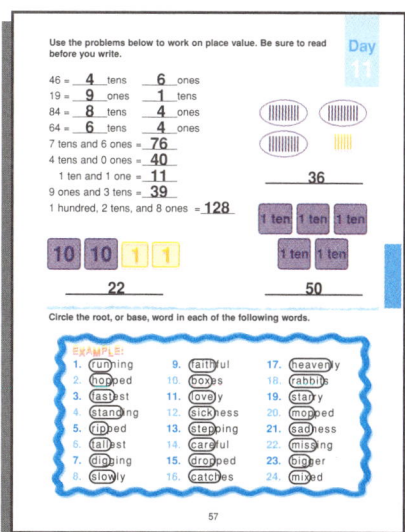
Page 57

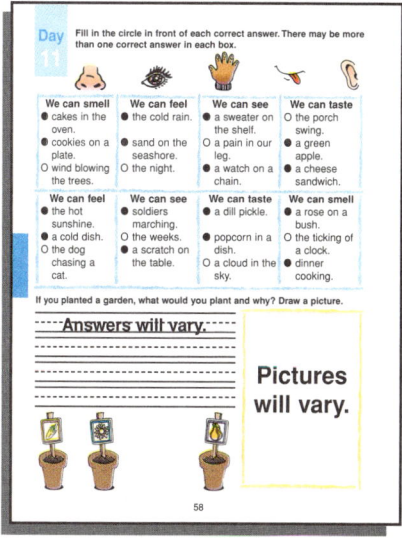
Page 58

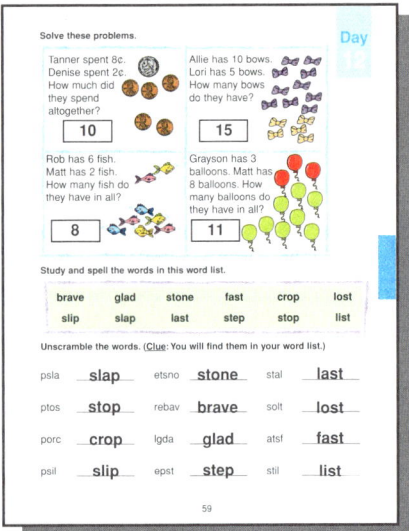

Page 59

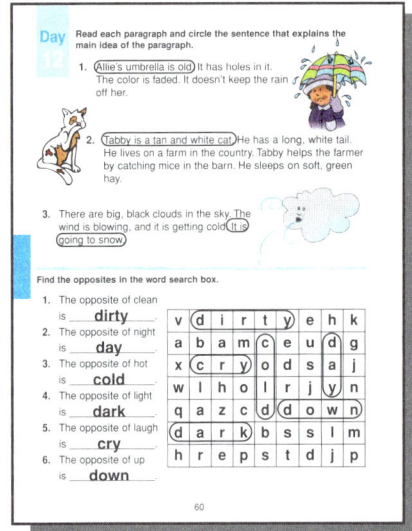

Page 60

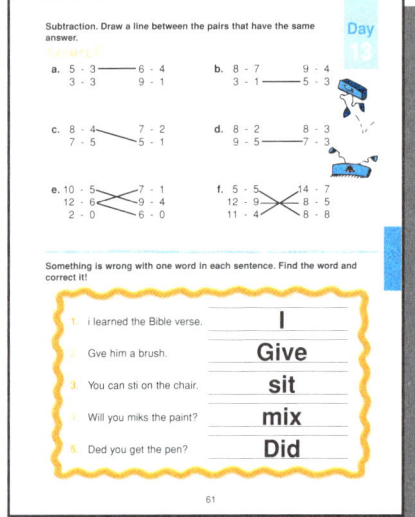

Page 61

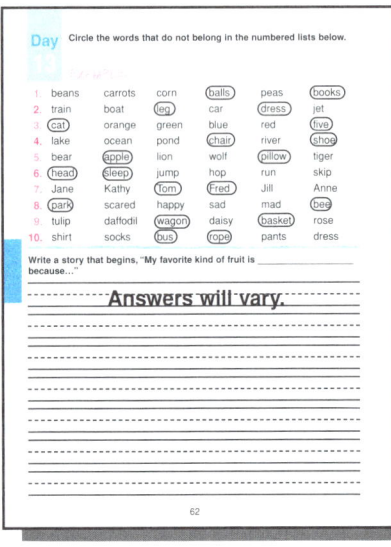

Page 62

Page 63

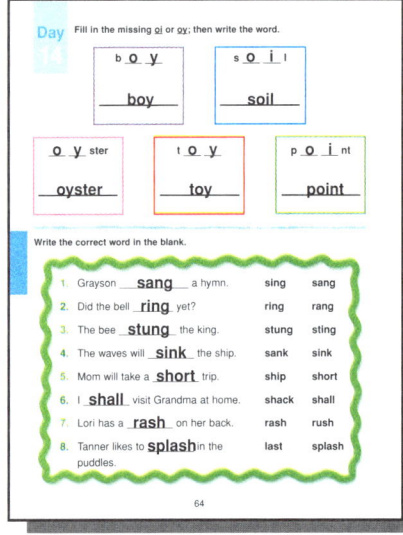

Page 64

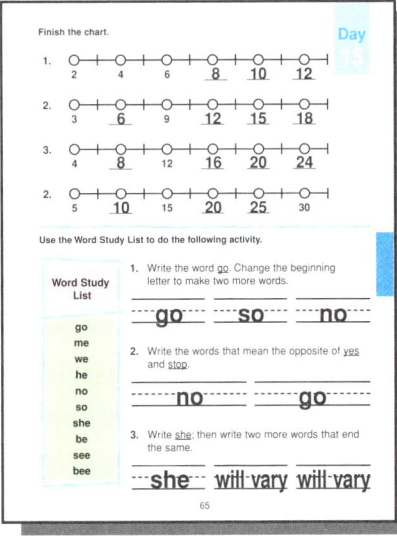

Page 65

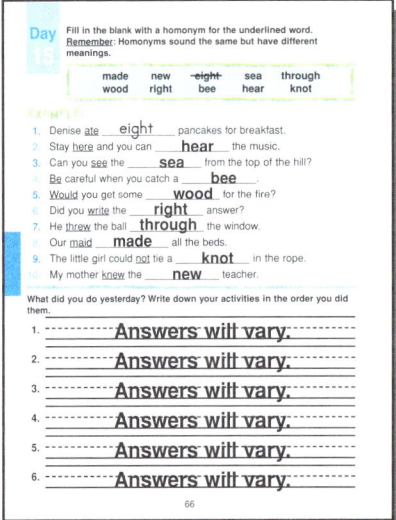

Page 66

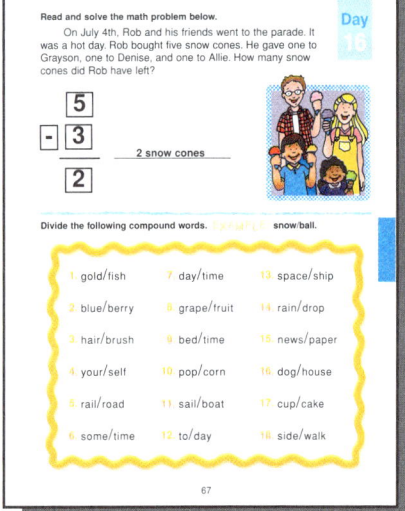

Page 67

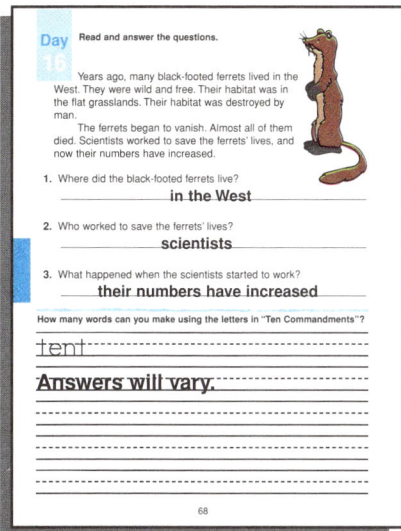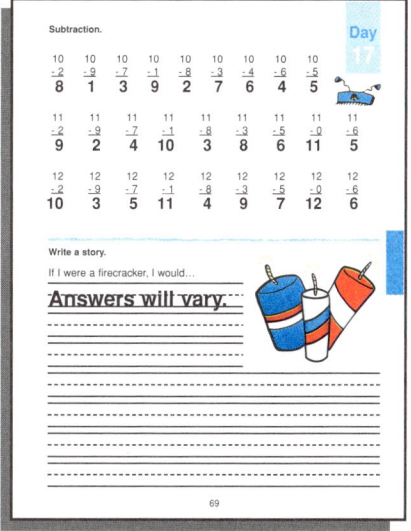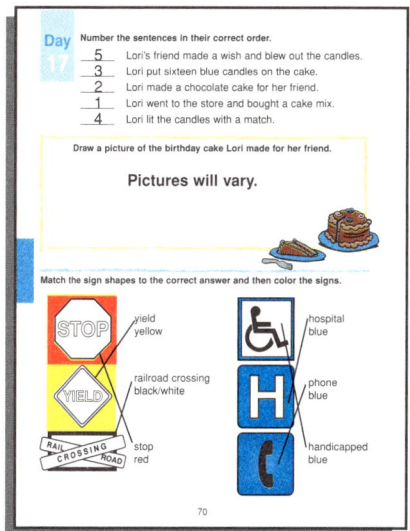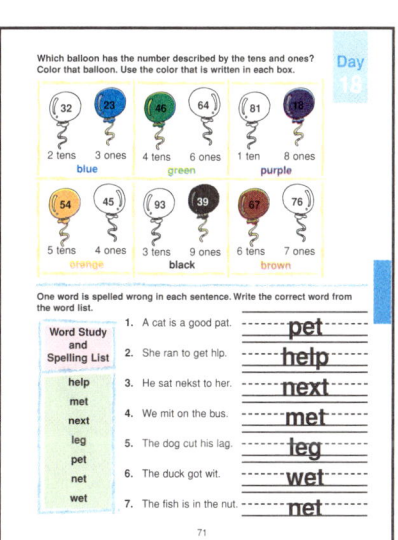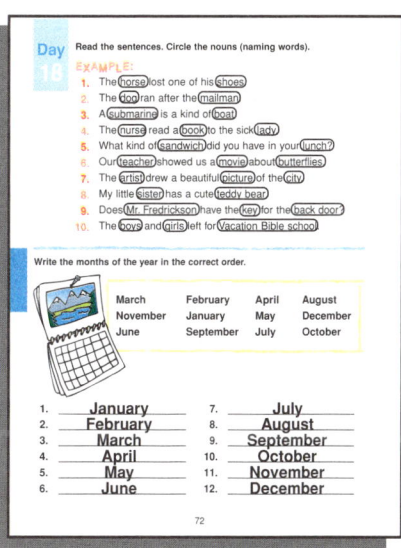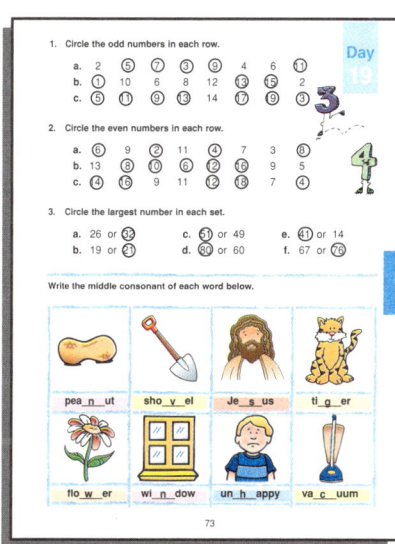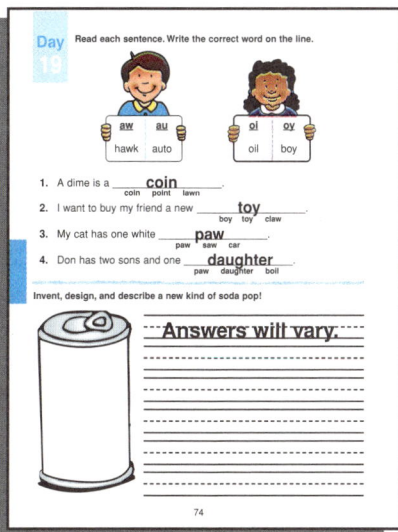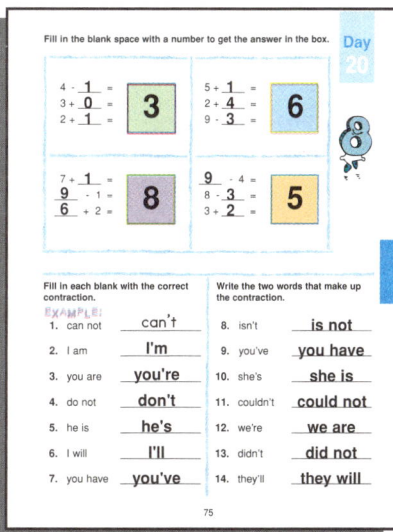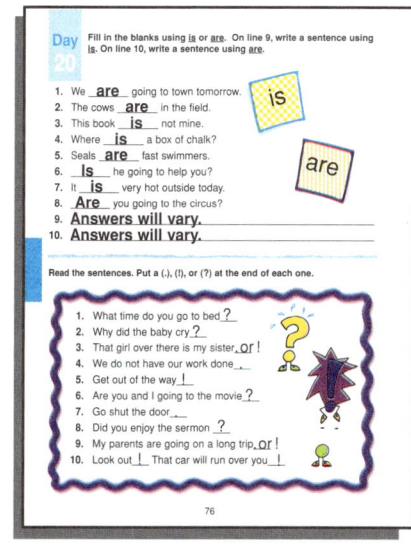

# Section 3

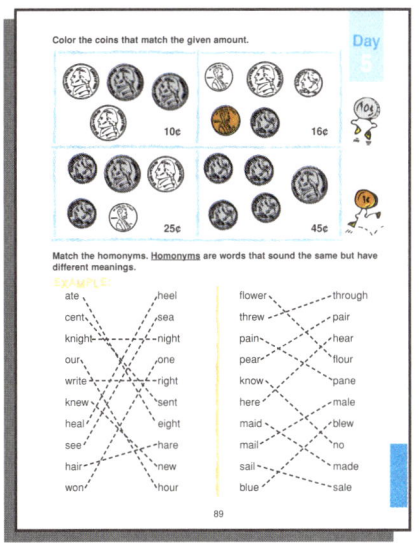
Page 89

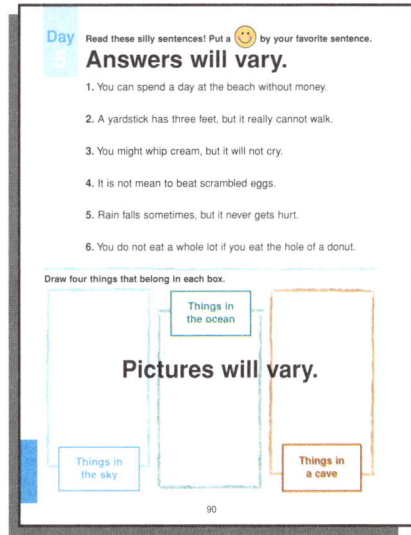
Page 90

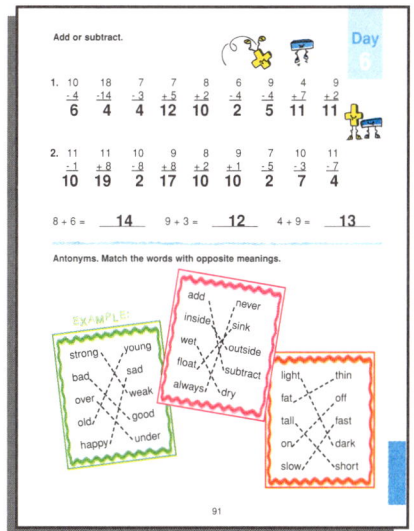
Page 91

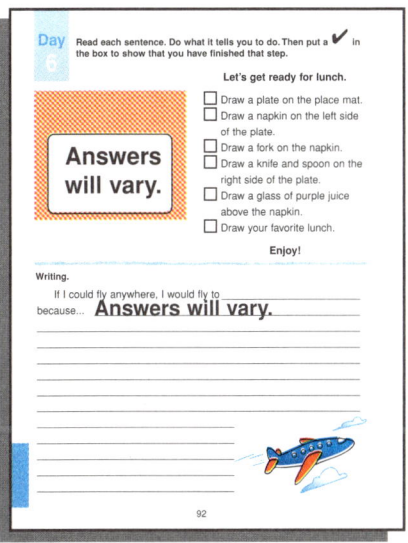
Page 92

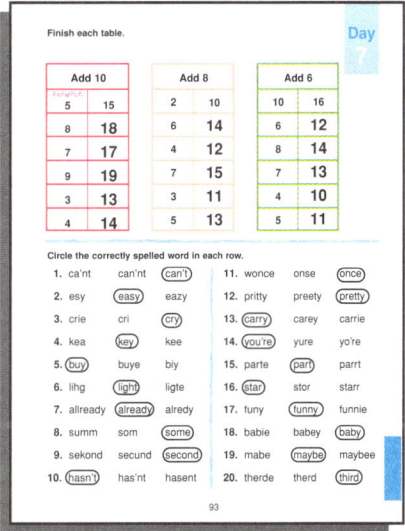
Page 93

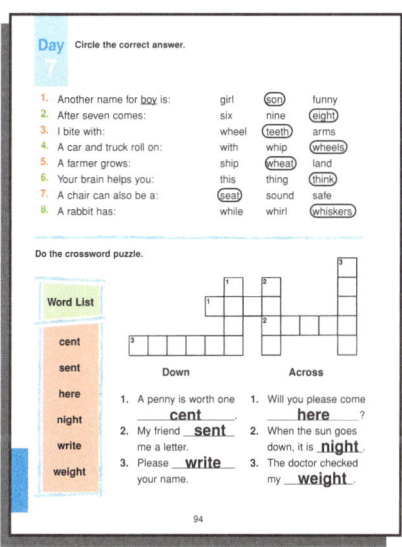
Page 94

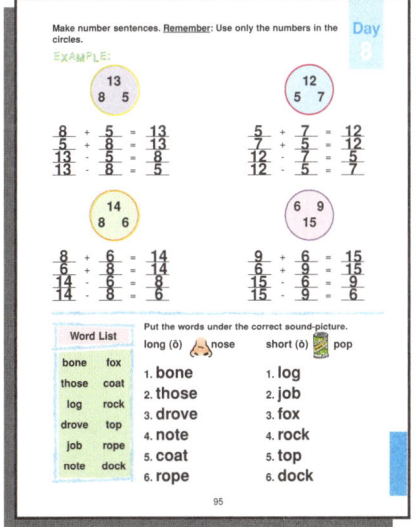
Page 95

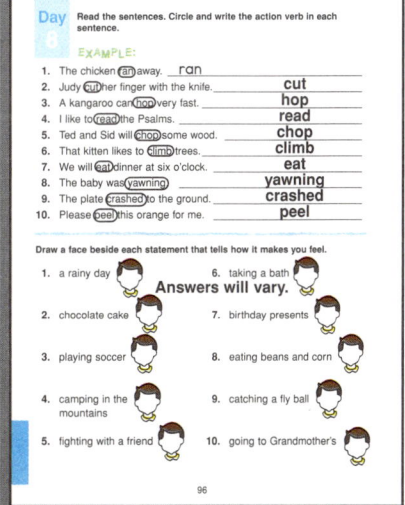
Page 96

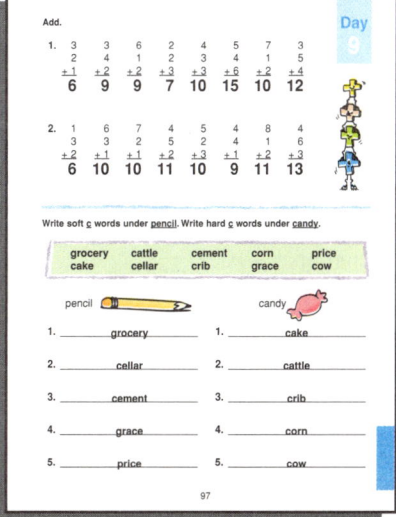
Page 97

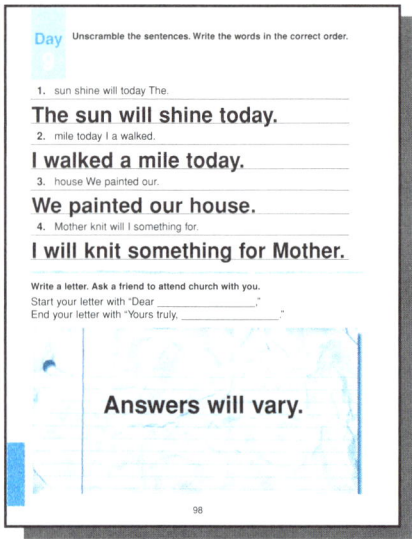

Page 98

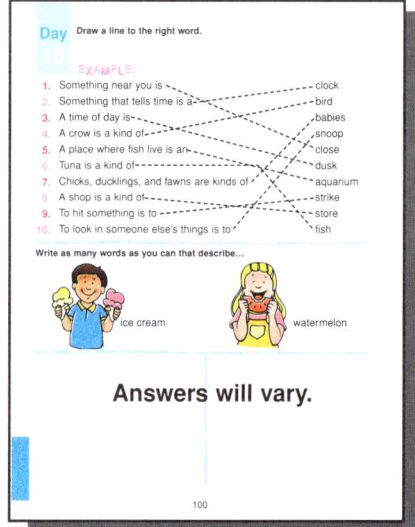

Page 99

Page 100

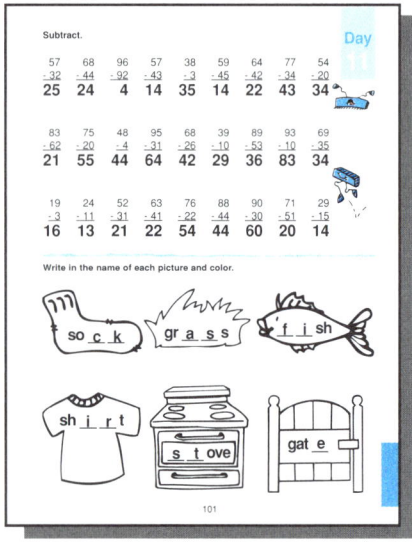

Page 101

Page 102

Page 103

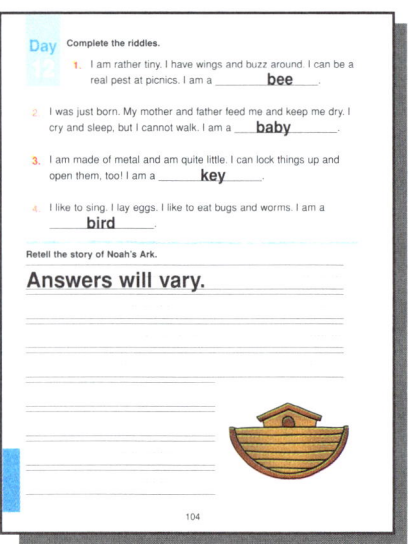

Page 104

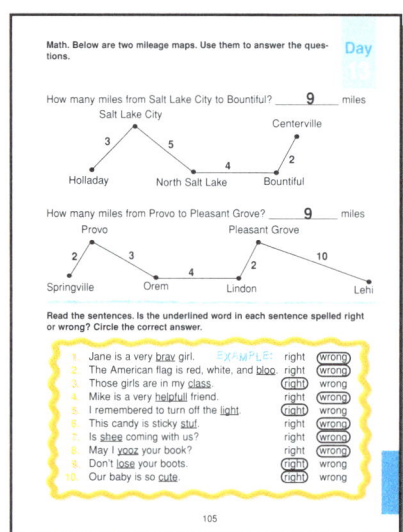

Page 105

Page 106

Page 107

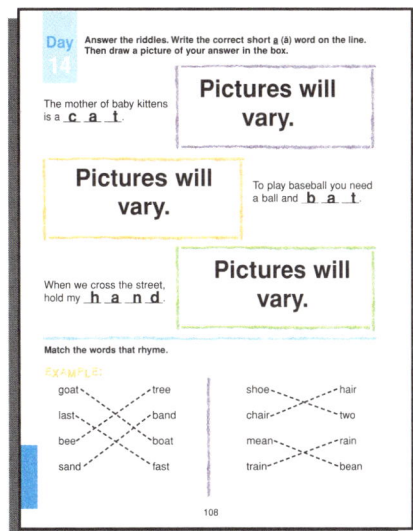

Page 108

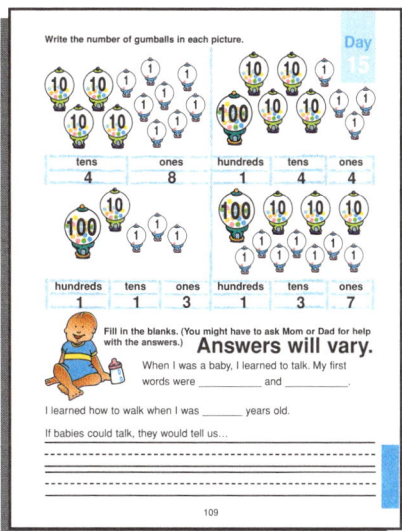

Page 109

Page 110

# Vacation Bible Camp

A special note to parents about Vacation Bible Camp.

As your child works through **Summer Bridge Activities**™ *for Young Christians* to maintain important academic skills, it is also vital for your child to further develop spiritual skills. That's why we have created this special bonus section for you to complete with your child. It features ten Bible lessons, one for each week of SBAYC. There are five Old Testament stories and five New Testament stories, with two pages of activities dedicated to each lesson. On the first page you'll find activities for days 1–3 of the week, with the scripture containing the Bible story, an everyday application, and a snack. The second page has days 4 and 5, which include a craft and a closing activity.

The Bible stories you and your child will learn about are the Creation, Noah's Ark, David and Goliath, Daniel and the Lions' Den, Jonah, the Birth of Jesus, the Good Samaritan, the Prodigal Son, Jesus and Zacchaeus, and Jesus' Death and Resurrection.

It is important for you and your child to complete the lessons together. By working together, you can help your child uncover the complete value in each lesson. All five of the week's activities focus on the Bible story and its lessons. Start day 1 by reading the Bible lesson straight from scripture; then help your child summarize the Bible story in words or pictures he or she can understand. On day 2 discuss and answer the everyday application question with your child. On day 3 prepare the special snack together. By day 4 your child should be picking up on the overall theme of the lesson as you prepare the craft. Complete the lesson on day 5 with the closing activity to reinforce the Bible message.

Before each week's lesson, review the activities to see that you have all the needed materials. Many of the snack and craft activities require basic kitchen items and craft materials, most of which you'll likely have around the house. Some of the activities themselves, such as using scissors and baking in the oven, will require adult supervision. But adult participation in all the activities will help both you and your child get the most from Summer Bridge Bible Camp.

You'll likely have as much fun attending Summer Bridge Bible Camp as your child—and you may even learn something!

www.summerbrains.com

© **Summer Bridge Activities**™

# Vacation Bible Camp

When you've completed ten weeks of Vacation Bible Camp, take some time to reflect on what you learned.

1. What was the most fun activity you completed? _____
   _____
   _____

2. What was the hardest activity you completed? _____
   _____
   _____

3. What did you like best about Vacation Bible Camp? _____
   _____
   _____

4. What was the most important thing you learned? _____
   _____
   _____

5. What can you share with others about what you learned? _____
   _____
   _____

# Vacation Bible Camp

## Week 1—The Creation

### Day 1—Bible Story Background

How did we get here on Earth?
Well, many years ago, God made the world and all the things in it. Everything He made was good.

> **Scripture** Read **Genesis 1:1–2:4**.
> Draw a picture of the Bible story, or tell the Bible story in your own words.

### Day 2—Everyday Application

Make a list of the things that God made on each day of Creation. Beside each creation, write why you are thankful for each of those things that were made so long ago.

### Day 3—Creation Cutouts with Sunshine Punch

Use nature cookie cutters (moon, star, animals, leaf, etc.) to cut out cheese, bread, and vegetables for cutout sandwiches. Serve the sandwiches with Sunshine Punch made from orange juice mixed with sparkling grape juice.

www.summerbrains.com

© Summer Bridge Activities™

# Vacation Bible Camp

## Day 4—Craft—Scrapbook of God's World

**Materials Needed:**
- hole punch
- construction paper
- scissors
- glue
- glitter glue pens (optional)
- fabric remnants or wrapping paper
- yarn or ribbon
- empty cereal box
- markers
- magazines
- stickers (optional)

**Assembly:**
Cut the front and back panels from the cereal box to make the covers for the scrapbook. Glue a fabric remnant or wrapping paper over each panel. Use the hole punch to make three holes along the left side of the front and back covers and three holes along the left side of seven sheets of construction paper, which will be used as the scrapbook pages. Assemble the scrapbook by lining up the holes and securing the pages with a length of yarn or ribbon. Label the pages Day 1, Day 2, etc. On each page, add pictures cut from magazines and drawn by hand that represent things that were made on each day of Creation. Enhance the pages by adding stickers or glitter glue designs. Use markers or glitter glue to embellish the cover by adding a catchy Creation title, such as "God's Crafty Creations" or "God's Awesome Handiwork." Share the scrapbook so others can see God's work!

## Day 5—Closing Activity

Go on a Creation nature walk. Head out to your backyard or local nature park—anyplace where you can see an abundance of God's creations. Notice the variety of things God made and the details found in nature, such as the very tall trees or the intricate patterns on a butterfly. Collect leaves, bugs, nuts, etc. When you get home, decorate a shoebox or other simple container by wrapping it in decorative paper, or use craft materials. On the lid add a title, such as "God's Creations." Put your finds in the box and put it in a special place. Add additional things as you go to new places in the magnificent world God has made.

# Vacation Bible Camp

## Week 2—Noah's Ark

**Week 2**

### Day 1—Bible Story Background

During Noah's time, the world was becoming a pretty bad place. However, even though many people chose to live sinful lives, Noah and his family continued to serve God. Because of Noah's faithfulness, God warned Noah that He was going to send a great flood. Noah soon found that faithfulness to God has great rewards.

> **Scripture** Read **Genesis 6:9–9:17**. Draw a picture of the Bible story, or tell the Bible story in your own words.

### Day 2—Everyday Application

While Noah was building the huge ark, he was probably teased by people who did not believe in God or in God's promise to send a flood. Sometimes it is hard to stand up for what you believe, especially when others tease you. What can you say to someone who is making fun of you for your beliefs?

### Day 3—Snack—Animal Crackers with Flood Water

Take several animal crackers and dip them into your favorite flavor of yogurt. Place the dipped crackers on a cookie sheet that has been covered with wax paper. Chill the crackers in the freezer for an hour. Serve the crackers with Flood Water made from milk and a few drops of blue food coloring.

www.summerbrains.com © Summer Bridge Activities™

# Vacation Bible Camp

## Day 4—Craft—Rainbow Door Decoration

**Materials Needed:**
- various colored party streamers (ideally red, orange, yellow, green, blue, indigo, and violet)
- poster board
- scissors
- glue
- yarn or ribbon
- white construction paper
- markers
- hole punch

**Assembly:**
Cut the poster board into a large arc, like a rainbow. Attach each streamer to the poster board by gluing one end at the bottom left corner. Twist the paper continually, applying glue as you go, until you reach the bottom right corner; then glue the other end of the streamer there. Stack each new color above the other. Cut a piece of white construction paper into a cloud shape. Write a special message on the cloud about being faithful to God. Write your own phrase or select a Bible verse to convey the message, such as "God watches over the faithful!" or "All the ways of the Lord are loving and faithful for those who keep the demands of his covenant" (Psalm 25:10). Attach the cloud to the rainbow by punching two holes in the bottom of the rainbow and two at the top of the cloud. String yarn or ribbon through the holes. Display the completed rainbow on your door.

## Day 5—Closing Activity

Reread the instructions God gave Noah on how to build the ark (**Genesis 6:14–21**). Using God's instructions, draw a scene showing what the completed ark may have looked like.

© Summer Bridge Activities™  
www.summerbrains.com

# Vacation Bible Camp

## Week 3—David and Goliath

**Week 3**

### Day 1—Bible Story Background

Goliath was the biggest soldier in the Philistines' army. For forty days, he challenged anyone in the Israelite army to come out and fight him. Boy, was he surprised when the soldier who accepted his challenge was just a kid! But this special soldier named David had an even bigger surprise in store for the giant.

> **Scripture** Read **1 Samuel 17:1–58**.
> Draw a picture of the Bible story, or tell the Bible story in your own words.

### Day 2—Everyday Application

Even though David was a young boy, he was not afraid of the giant Goliath because David knew that God was fighting with him. David even refused to wear armor to battle Goliath. Find a Bible verse that will remind you of the strength and protection God can give you when you are afraid or must overcome a tough situation.
(Hint: Use your Bible's concordance for help.)

### Day 3—Snack—"Stone" Fruits with Sling-Zing Punch

Use a melon baller to cut various fruits, such as bananas, apples, peaches, and pears, into round "stone" shapes. Serve the fruit with Sling-Zing Punch made from fruit juice mixed with lemon-lime soda served over crushed ice.

www.summerbrains.com

© Summer Bridge Activities™

# Vacation Bible Camp

## Day 4—Craft—Shield of God's Protection

**Materials Needed:**
- aluminum foil
- foam board
- craft knife
- construction paper
- scissors
- markers
- strong glue
- glitter glue pens (optional)

**Assembly:**
Cut the foam board into the shape of a shield. Glue sections of aluminum foil to the shield to make it look like metal. Cut out various shapes, such as triangles and squares, from construction paper. On the paper shapes, write Bible verses that tell about God's protection and love for you. Place your favorite protection verse, such as "We wait in hope for the Lord, he is our help and our shield. Psalm 33:20," on the middle of the shield. Attach the rest of the verses. Finish the shield by decorating it with additional designs using construction paper, glitter glue, or other craft materials.

## Day 5—Closing Activity

Adapted from **Psalm 28:7** "The Lord is my strength and shield; my heart trusts in him, and I am helped." Sung to the tune of "Itsy, Bitsy Spider."

The Lord is my strength and my protecting shield.

My heart trusts in Him, in Him, on—ly Him.

And I am helped, yes, He shows me the way.

The Lord is my strength and shield—each and every day.

(* indicates emphasis)

# Vacation Bible Camp

## Week 4—Daniel and the Lions' Den

**Week 4**

### Day 1—Bible Story Background

Daniel was a man of God who would not stop worshipping the Lord, even when the king made this against the law. Daniel trusted God so much that he was not even afraid to be thrown into a lions' den.

> **Scripture** Read **Daniel 6:1–28**. Draw a picture of the Bible story, or tell the Bible story in your own words.

### Day 2—Everyday Application

Proverbs 3:5 tells us to "trust in the Lord with all your heart." The Bible makes it clear that Daniel put his trust in God. Think of a time when you were having trouble. Did you ask God for His help? The next time you are in a tough situation, what can you do to show that you have put your trust in the Lord?

### Day 3—Snack—Lion Pizza with Luscious Lemonade

Roll out a package of prepared pizza dough onto a floured surface. With a plastic knife, cut a big circle (for the lion's face) and several small triangles (for the lion's mane). Place the triangles around the circle. Cover the face portion with pizza sauce, and use your favorite pizza toppings to form the lion's eyes, nose, mouth, and ears. Bake the pizza dough according to the package directions. Serve with Luscious Lemonade made from three cups water, one cup lemon juice, and sugar to taste.

www.summerbrains.com

© Summer Bridge Activities™

# Vacation Bible Camp

## Day 4—Craft—Loveable Lion

**Materials Needed:**
- white paper plate
- crayons or markers
- macaroni
- construction paper
- scissors
- dark yarn
- glue

**Assembly:**
Make the lion's face by coloring the paper plate light brown. Cut the edges of the plate with jagged edges to imitate a furry mane. Glue several pieces of macaroni to the lion's mane. The lion's face can be made by drawing it or by gluing construction paper scraps to form its eyes, nose, mouth, and ears. Attach long strips of dark yarn to make its whiskers. Complete the lion by adding a collar made from construction paper. On the collar, write a phrase about God's love, such as "God is love—no lion," or "God's love is puuurrrrrfect."

## Day 5—Closing Activity

Daniel 6:21 simply tells us that God sent an angel to shut the mouths of the lions. Draw a scene showing in detail how you think Daniel and the closed-mouth lions would have looked in the den.

# Vacation Bible Camp

## Week 5—Jonah and the Big Fish

### Day 1—Bible Story Background

God wanted Jonah to go preach to the people of Nineveh, but Jonah did not want to go. Jonah tried to run away from God by hopping on a ship and sailing away from Nineveh. Jonah soon learned that God was not going to take "no" for an answer.

> **Scripture** Read **Jonah 1:1–4:10**. Draw a picture of the Bible story, or tell the Bible story in your own words.

### Day 2—Everyday Application

Jonah tried to hide from God because he did not want to preach in Nineveh. We know that it is impossible to hide from God because He is everywhere. When you have a task to do that you do not want to do (but know you should), what can you do to make the job go better?

### Day 3—Snack—Whale of a Cookie with Jonah Juice

Roll out and flour a package of prepared sugar cookie dough, and cut out a large whale or fish shape. Bake according to the package directions. Frost and decorate your "whale of a cookie" with icing and your favorite sweet toppings. Serve with Jonah Juice made from your favorite fruit juice mixed with sparkling water.

www.summerbrains.com

© Summer Bridge Activities™

# Vacation Bible Camp

## Day 4—Craft—Whale of a Mobile

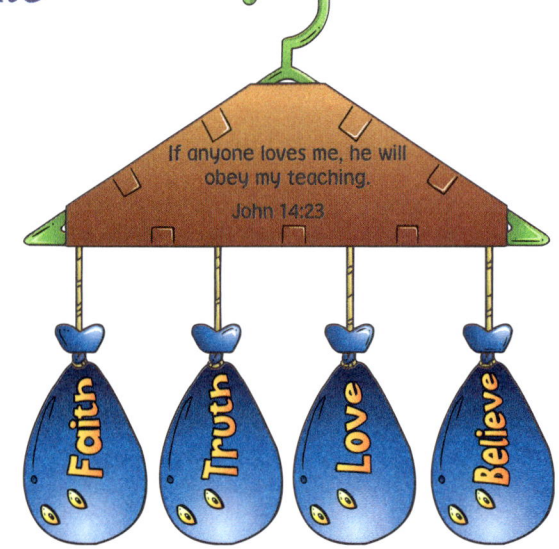

**Materials Needed:**
- round balloons
- construction paper
- scissors
- clear tape
- craft googly eyes
- yarn or ribbon
- coat hanger
- markers

**Assembly:**
Blow up several round balloons to form the whale bodies. Use clear tape to attach a tail cut from construction paper to each balloon. Add two craft googly eyes to each whale. Write words that reflect faith in God, such as "trust" and "love," on each whale. Attach the whales to the coat hanger by tying one end of a length of yarn or ribbon to each tail (where the balloon is tied off) and tying the other end to the coat hanger. Cut a piece of construction paper to fit over the open portion of the coat hanger. Use clear tape to attach the paper to both sides of the hanger. On each side of the paper, write a message or verse about being obedient to God, such as John 14:23 "If anyone loves me, he will obey my teaching." Hang the completed mobile from a ceiling or doorway.

## Day 5—Closing Activity

Memorize Jonah 2:2 "In my distress I called to the Lord, and he answered me. From the depths of the grave I called for help, and you listened to my cry." Think of this verse when you are troubled and need God's help.

# Vacation Bible Camp
## Week 6—The Birth of Jesus

**Week 6**

### Day 1—Bible Story Background

Many years ago, a very special baby was born. This child was so special that shepherds who heard of His birth traveled far to see Him. Also, three very wise men came to bring Him special gifts. That baby's name was Jesus—the same Jesus that we love and worship today.

> **Scripture** Read **Luke 2:1–20**, **Matthew 2:1–12**. Draw a picture of the Bible story, or tell the Bible story in your own words.

### Day 2—Everyday Application

When the wise men finally saw Jesus, they presented Him with beautiful gifts. What kinds of "gifts" can you give to Jesus?

### Day 3—Snack—Sweet Gifts with Magi Milk

Use three graham crackers broken in half to make a box. Use prepared frosting to carefully attach the box sides together. Chill the assembled box in the freezer for about an hour on a cookie sheet covered with wax paper. Cover the top and sides of the box with more frosting. Add a bow made with a piece of skinny licorice. Serve with Magi Milk made from milk and chocolate syrup.

www.summerbrains.com © Summer Bridge Activities™

# Vacation Bible Camp

## Day 4—Craft—Sleeping Sheep Watching over Jesus

**Materials Needed:**
- newspaper
- cotton balls
- strong glue
- four black craft pompoms
- white spray paint or white craft paint and paintbrushes
- stapler
- scissors
- two marbles or buttons
- markers

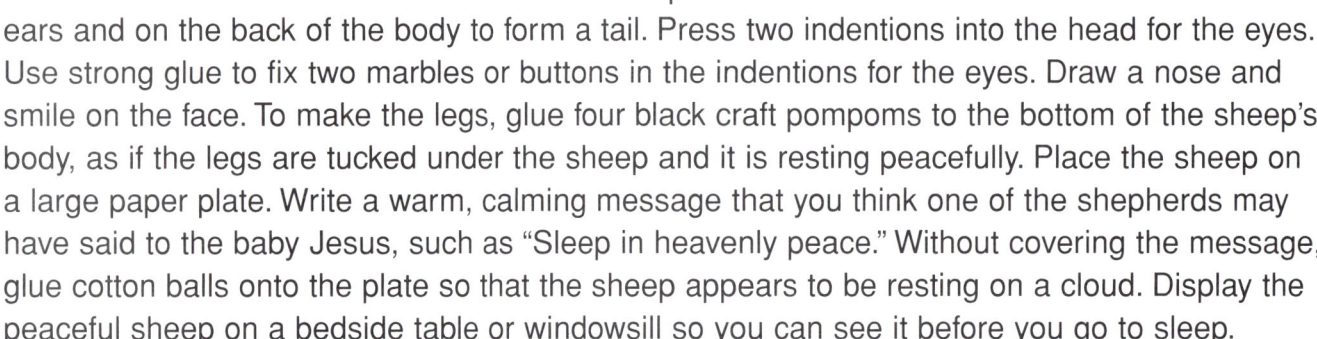

Sleep in heavenly peace.

**Assembly:**
Ball up a large piece of newspaper to form the sheep's body and a small piece to form its head. Attach the body and head with a stapler. Paint the head and body white. Glue a few cotton balls on each side of the sheep's face to make ears and on the back of the body to form a tail. Press two indentions into the head for the eyes. Use strong glue to fix two marbles or buttons in the indentions for the eyes. Draw a nose and smile on the face. To make the legs, glue four black craft pompoms to the bottom of the sheep's body, as if the legs are tucked under the sheep and it is resting peacefully. Place the sheep on a large paper plate. Write a warm, calming message that you think one of the shepherds may have said to the baby Jesus, such as "Sleep in heavenly peace." Without covering the message, glue cotton balls onto the plate so that the sheep appears to be resting on a cloud. Display the peaceful sheep on a bedside table or windowsill so you can see it before you go to sleep.

## Day 5—Closing Activity

At Christmas we celebrate Jesus' birthday. Write the baby Jesus a birthday card telling Him what His birth means to you.

© Summer Bridge Activities™                   www.summerbrains.com

# Vacation Bible Camp

## Week 7—The Good Samaritan

**Week 7**

## Day 1—Bible Story Background

Jesus often told stories to teach lessons. In one, He told about a man who was hurt very badly and a stranger who was kind to him. The stranger who showed mercy to the hurt man is a wonderful example of how to treat others.

> **Scripture** Read **Luke 10:25–37**.
> Draw a picture of the Bible story, or tell the Bible story in your own words.

## Day 2—Everyday Application

Have you ever shown kindness to someone you didn't know very well? What are some ways that you can show kindness to others?

## Day 3—Snack—Coin Cookies with Mercy Milkshakes

Mix a few drops of yellow food coloring into some ready-made vanilla pudding. Dip vanilla wafers into the pudding; then place the covered wafers on a cookie sheet that has been covered with wax paper. Chill the wafers in the freezer for an hour. Serve the wafers with a Mercy Milkshake made from a glass of milk and a scoop of your favorite ice cream blended together.

www.summerbrains.com

© Summer Bridge Activities™

# Vacation Bible Camp

## Day 4—Craft—Mercy Money Purse

**Materials Needed:**
- paper lunch bag
- ribbon
- cereal box
- yellow spray paint or craft paint and paintbrushes
- glitter glue pens
- scissors
- markers

**Assembly:**
On the outside of the paper bag write "Mercy Money." Crumple the paper bag several times into a ball to soften it. Make several coins by cutting out circles (approximately two inches in diameter) from a cereal box. Paint each circle, and highlight each coin's edge using glitter glue. When the coins have dried, write a reminder on each one that tells you how to treat your neighbors. Place the coins in the bag, and tie a ribbon around it to secure it. When you are having trouble showing kindness to someone, pull out one of the coins so that you'll remember how Jesus instructed us to treat others.

## Day 5—Closing Activity

Sing this song to tell others how much you care for them.
Sung to the tune "Happy Birthday to You."

    *            *
I will respect and love you.

   *         *
I will care for you, too!

     *            *
For you are my neigh—bor,

  *        *
and I do love you!

(* indicates emphasis)

© Summer Bridge Activities™     www.summerbrains.com

# Vacation Bible Camp

## Week 8—The Prodigal Son

### Day 1—Bible Story Background

Jesus told another very good story. This one was about a young man who took his inheritance from his father and then went off and wasted it. Fortunately for him, the young man had a father much like our heavenly Father—one who loves us and will forgive us, no matter what we do.

> **Scripture** Read **Luke 15:11–32**. Draw a picture of the Bible story, or tell the Bible story in your own words.

### Day 2—Everyday Application

The older brother in the story was upset that his younger brother was given such a wonderful welcome home. He didn't understand why his brother was being greeted with such love. What would you tell the older brother to help him understand why his father treated his younger son in such a loving way?

### Day 3—Snack—Sapphire Welcome Rings with Purple Prodigal Punch

Make blueberry muffins using a prepared box mix. After the muffins have cooled, make a hole in the middle of each muffin by inserting the end of a wooden spoon (you can eat any muffin holes you create). Serve the muffin rings with Purple Prodigal Punch made from grape juice mixed with cranberry juice and served over crushed ice.

www.summerbrains.com © Summer Bridge Activities™

## Vacation Bible Camp

### Week 8

### Welcome Home Robe

- dress shirt (larger is better)
- scissors
- fabric markers or permanent markers
- plastic soda caps
- glue
- craft paints and paintbrushes
- glitter glue pens
- markers

**Assembly:**
Cut the collar off the shirt. Add "jewels" to the shirt by gluing painted plastic soda caps to the existing buttons. Add designs using glitter glue or markers around the neck, the front of the shirt, and the cuffs. On the back of the shirt use fabric paint or markers to write a Bible verse that talks about our heavenly Father, such as "I will be a Father to you, and you will be my sons and daughters" (2 Corinthians 6:18). Wear the robe and share the story of the Prodigal Son with a family member or friend.

### Day 5 — Closing Activity

Matthew 6:9–13 is known as the Lord's Prayer. This prayer was written as an example of how we should pray. Take time to memorize these verses and to follow this prayer as an example when you talk to the Lord in prayer.

# Vacation Bible Camp

## Week 9—Jesus and Zacchaeus

### Day 1—Bible Story Background

Zacchaeus was a tax collector. Back in Jesus' day, tax collectors were known to cheat people out of their money. Zacchaeus was one of those kinds of tax collectors. But with Jesus' love, anyone can change their ways!

> **Scripture** Read **Luke 19:1–10**.
> Draw a picture of the Bible story, or tell the Bible story in your own words.

### Day 2—Everyday Application

When Jesus spoke kindly to Zacchaeus and gladly went to his house, the people were surprised because they thought Zacchaeus was a sinner. How should you treat other people who you know may not be Christians?

### Day 3—Snack—Sycamore Tree Snacks with Forgiveness Fruit Drink

Stick a group of four or five skinny pretzel sticks in a large cube of cheese to form the trunk of a tree. Place another block of cheese at the top of the pretzel trunk. Stick individual pretzel sticks in the top cheese cube to make tree limbs. Serve with Forgiveness Fruit Drink made from 2/3 cup lemon juice, 1/3 cup orange juice, and 1/4 cup sugar mixed together and served over ice cubes.

www.summerbrains.com © Summer Bridge Activities™

# ion Bible Camp

## Week 9

### ctable Love Coins

**Modeling Dough Ingredients**
2 cups baking soda
1 1/4 cups water
1 cup cornstarch
rolling pin
waxed paper
round cookie cutter    toothpick

- paintbrushes
- pens
- markers
- yarn or ribbon

**Assembly:**
Prepare the modeling dough by combining baking soda and cornstarch. Add the water. Mix thoroughly in a saucepan and stir over medium heat till mixture comes to a low boil. Continue until a dough consistency is reached. Turn the dough onto a plate covered with a damp cloth. Refrigerate for half an hour. Knead the dough 3 to 4 minutes. Flour the wax paper. Roll the dough out 1/4 inch thick. Cut with the round cookie cutter to make coin shapes. Make a hole in the top of each dough coin with a toothpick. Let the dough coins dry for several hours. Heat the oven to 350 degrees. Place the coins onto a cookie sheet. When the tops of the coins appear dry (a few minutes), turn each over with a spatula and dry the backs. When the coins have cooled, paint each one gold. Decorate each coin's edge with glitter glue. In the center of each coin, write a Bible verse or reminder about how to forgive and treat others, as Jesus did with Zacchaeus. String a length of yarn or ribbon through the hole in each circle. Hang the completed coins in various places throughout the house as friendly reminders about forgiveness.

## Day 5—Closing Activity

Luke 19:3–4 provides a basic description of little Zacchaeus trying to see Jesus from up in a tree. Draw a picture showing how you think this scene would have looked.

© Summer Bridge Activities™

www.summerbrains.com

# Vacation Bible Camp

**Week 10**

## Week 10—The Death and Resurrection of Jesus Christ

### Day 1—Bible Story Background

Jesus is our Savior. That means that He died for our sins. It is all of our sins that placed Jesus on the cross. But the best part about Him being our Savior is that not only did He die, but He also rose again!

> **Scripture** Read **Mark 15:22–16:1–20**. Draw a picture of the Bible story, or tell the Bible story in your own words.

### Day 2—Everyday Application

Not everybody knows the true story of how Jesus died for each of us on the cross and rose again. Share the story of His love and sacrifice with someone that you know.

> **Grades 1–2, 2–3** Be sure to have your Bible with you to show the specific verses that tell these important events.

### Day 3—Snack—He-Rolled-away-the-Stone Sweet Rolls with Spiced Tea

Bake a batch of pre-made sweet rolls according to the package directions. Serve the rolls with Spiced Tea made from decaffeinated iced tea mixed with 1/4 cup sugar, 1/4 teaspoon cinnamon, 1/4 teaspoon ground cloves, and 1/8 teaspoon ginger.

www.summerbrains.com

© Summer Bridge Activities™

# Vacation Bible Camp

## Day 4—Craft—3-D Cross Centerpiece

**Materials Needed:**
- clean, empty milk carton
- toothpicks
- sticky tack
- markers or craft paint and paintbrushes
- glitter glue pens (optional)
- scissors

**Assembly:**
Cut the milk carton so that you have two large, clean panels. Cut the panels into equal-sized cross shapes. Decorate one side of each of the cross shapes with markers or craft paints. Add additional embellishments with glitter glue, if desired. Leave space on both sides of the cross shapes to write a verse about Jesus' love for us, such as, "For God so loved the world that he gave his one and only Son, that whoever believes in him shall not perish but have eternal life" (John 3:16). To connect the two cross panels, place a small ball of sticky tack in each of the corners. Line up the two cross panels and attach them by inserting a toothpick in each of the matching pieces of sticky tack. This will create a 3-D effect, and your cross can stand and be placed on a table or other surface to show others.

## Day 5—Closing Activity

Sing this song to tell others how much you care for them.
Sung to the tune of "Row, Row, Row Your Boat."

   \*   \*   \*   \*
Roll, roll, roll a—way

       \*   \*    \*
He rolled a—way the stone.

   \*   \*   \*   \*
Je—sus died and rose a—gain

    \*    \*   \*
So heaven could be our home.

(\* indicates emphasis)

© Summer Bridge Activities™     www.summerbrains.com

# Activities for Addition and Subtraction Cards

Use the flashcards to practice addition and subtraction facts from 0-10. Make piles of facts you know and facts you need some help on. Review the pile of cards you need help on until you are an addition/subtraction expert!

Each card shows an addition or subtraction fact on each side. On the opposite side of the card, the answer to the equation is shown in the lower left-hand corner. Addition facts are colored magenta and the subtraction facts are shown in green.

## Enrichment Activities for Sound Cards

Assess what your child knows and understands, then use only those activities your child needs.

Two different types of lowercase "a's" are included. You may want to find out which type of "a" your child will be using at his/her school. You could also identify the two different types of "a's" by stating that "a" is the one we use to write with and "a" is the "book a"—the one we find in many reading books.

Parents, when you are working with the letter sounds and the sound blending process, you may exaggerate the letter sounds, but be careful you don't distort them.

When working with the letter sounds, sound blending, and word recognition, you need to help your child learn that these sound words usually work this way but there are words that "do not follow the rules."

## Consonants

1. Consonant recognition—Start with the consonant sound cards first. Explain that the letters of the alphabet have letter names and letter sounds. Identify the consonant letters and tell your child that these are called consonants because they usually have only one sound.

2. Take just a few (1 to 3) sound cards at a time. Identify the letter name on the front and the sound picture on the back. Exaggerate the beginning sound. Now, say two words to help your child choose the word that starts with the same beginning sound as the sound card you are working with. When he/she becomes familiar and successful with this process, you can increase the number of sound cards you are working with.

3. Give your child 3 to 5 sound cards. Say a word or name an object and have him/her hold up the sound card beginning with the same sound.

4. Play the slap game. Say the sounds and/or words and have your child identify the sound card by slapping it.

5. As the child gets better at this, have him/her say a sound and/or word and see if he/she can beat you at the slap game mentioned in the activity above.

6. Have your child label his/her toys by their beginning sound. Give him/her small pieces of paper. Have him/her write down the letter or sound he/she thinks it begins with and place the paper by the toy or on top of it. See if the child can find 2 or more toys that begin with the same sound.

7. Activities 2 through 6 can be used to identify and understand ending sounds (the sound the objects end with).

## Vowels

1. Explain to your child that vowels have more than one sound. Identify and teach the short vowel sounds before proceeding with the long vowel sounds.

2. Start with the short "a" vowel sound card. Show your child the apple on the back. Say the word "apple," then say it again, exaggerating the "a" sound. Have your child repeat the procedure, then say, "Apple begins with the short 'a' sound."

3. Say 2 or more words and help your child identify those words that begin with the short "a" sound. (Example: ax, astronaut, octopus.)

4. Tell your child there are a lot of words that have the short "a" sound in them, such as "pat," "can," and "man." Next, say two or more words, varying short vowel and long vowel sounds. Then help your child identify which words have the short "a" sound in them.

5. Help your child learn to sound out or sound blend very simple short "a" words (example: can, fat, nap) by writing them on paper, chalkboard, magic slate, cards, etc.

6. Use activities for the other short vowel sounds of e, i, o, and u.

7. Use the consonant sound cards with the short vowel sound cards to put together simple words.

EXAMPLE:

Using the first letter sound of picture side of card.

Using the letters on the other side of card to make the word "man."

8. Follow the same procedure as #7, only this time change just the beginning sound or letter card to make new words (rhyming words). (Example: man, fan, ran, can, etc.)

9. Follow the same procedure as #7, only this time change just the ending sound or letter card to make new words. (Example: man, map, mat, etc.)

10. Follow the same procedure as #7, only this time change just the short vowel sound or letter card to make new words. (Example: pan, pen, pin, etc.)

11. Say a short vowel word and see if your child can use the sound or letter cards to make the word. Whenever time permits, have your child extend this activity by recording the word on a piece of paper.

12. Word dictation—give your child a pencil and paper. Say a simple word he/she has previously worked on and have your child write it down. Praise your child for his/her efforts and check the word/words frequently as you do this activity.

# Long Vowels

1. Talk to your child about how long vowels "say their own name," or sound like the name of the letter. Also, help him/her to understand that when a vowel "says its own name," it usually needs another vowel with it—for example, "cake," "boat," "teeth."

2. Parents, you can use most of the activities listed for short vowel words for long vowel words with a few minor changes.

| 0 + 0 | 1 + 0 | 2 + 0 | 3 + 0 |
|---|---|---|---|
| 7 | 8 | 9 | 10 |
| 4 + 0 | 5 + 0 | 6 + 0 | 7 + 0 |
| 3 | 4 | 5 | 6 |
| 8 + 0 | 9 + 0 | 10 + 0 | 1 + 1 |
| 9 | 0 | 1 | 2 |

| | | | |
|---|---|---|---|
| 10<br>− 0<br><br>3 | 10<br>− 1<br><br>2 | 10<br>− 2<br><br>1 | 10<br>− 3<br><br>0 |
| 10<br>− 4<br><br>7 | 10<br>− 5<br><br>6 | 10<br>− 6<br><br>5 | 10<br>− 7<br><br>4 |
| 10<br>− 8<br><br>2 | 10<br>− 9<br><br>10 | 10<br>−10<br><br>9 | 9<br>− 0<br><br>8 |

| 2 | 2 | 3 | 3 |
|---|---|---|---|
| +1 | +2 | +1 | +2 |
| 5 | 6 | 7 | 8 |

| 3 | 4 | 4 | 4 |
|---|---|---|---|
| +3 | +1 | +2 | +3 |
| 1 | 2 | 3 | 4 |

| 4 | 5 | 5 | 5 |
|---|---|---|---|
| +4 | +1 | +2 | +3 |
| 6 | 7 | 8 | 0 |

| 9 − 1 | 9 − 2 | 9 − 3 | 9 − 4 |
|---|---|---|---|
| 5 | 4 | 4 | 3 |

| 9 − 5 | 9 − 6 | 9 − 7 | 9 − 8 |
|---|---|---|---|
| 7 | 6 | 5 | 6 |

| 9 − 9 | 8 − 0 | 8 − 1 | 8 − 2 |
|---|---|---|---|
| 8 | 7 | 6 | 8 |

| | | | |
|---|---|---|---|
| 5<br>+ 4<br><br>2 | 5<br>+ 5<br><br>3 | 6<br>+ 1<br><br>4 | 6<br>+ 2<br><br>5 |
| 6<br>+ 3<br><br>6 | 6<br>+ 4<br><br>7 | 7<br>+ 1<br><br>0 | 7<br>+ 2<br><br>1 |
| 7<br>+ 3<br><br>2 | 8<br>+ 1<br><br>3 | 8<br>+ 2<br><br>4 | 9<br>+ 1<br><br>5 |

| 8 − 3 | 8 − 4 | 8 − 5 | 8 − 6 |
|---|---|---|---|
| 8 | 7 | 10 | 9 |
| 8 − 7 | 8 − 8 | 7 − 0 | 7 − 1 |
| 9 | 8 | 10 | 9 |
| 7 − 2 | 7 − 3 | 7 − 4 | 7 − 5 |
| 10 | 10 | 9 | 10 |

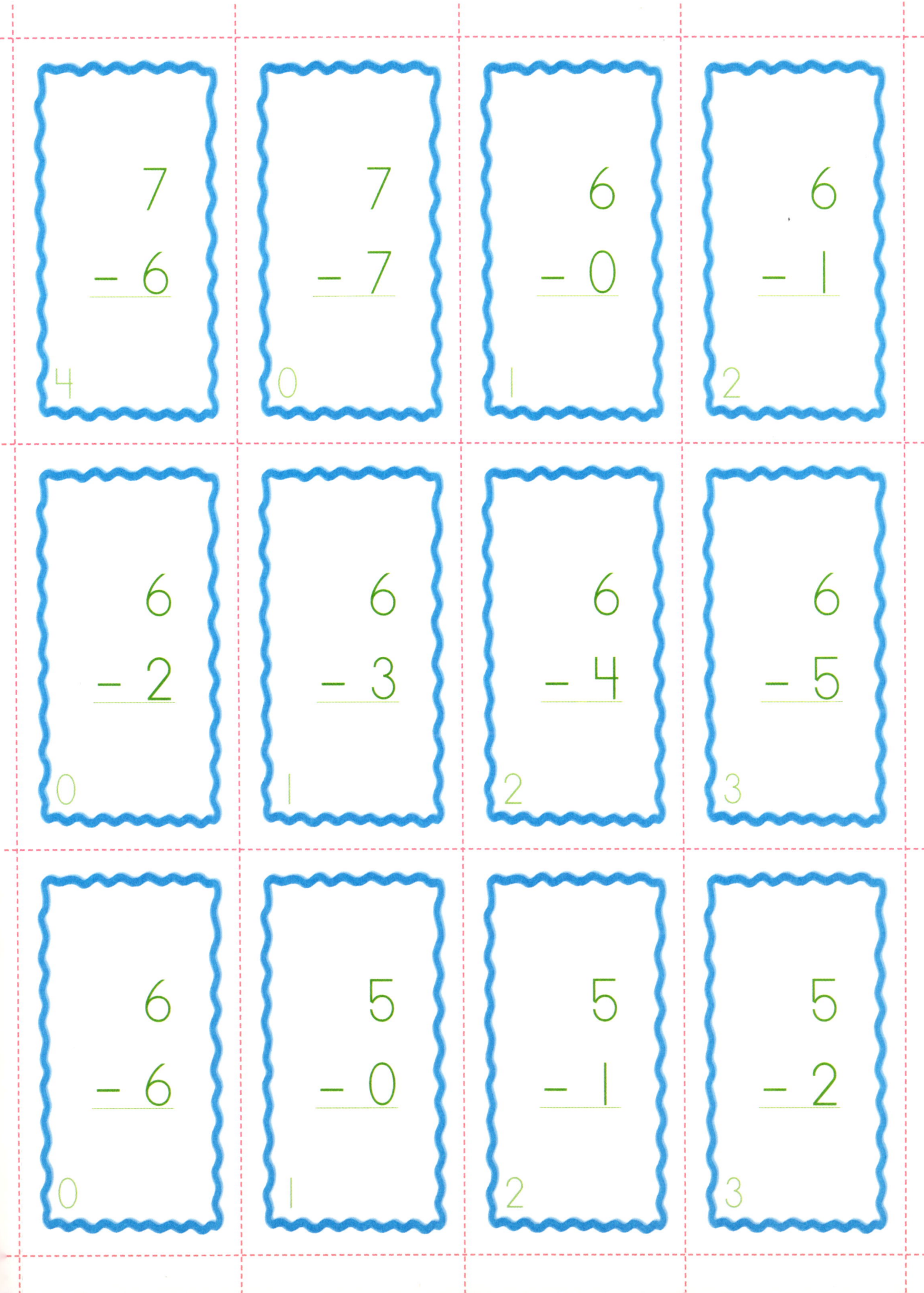

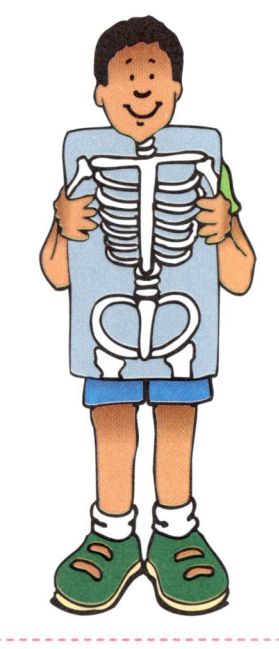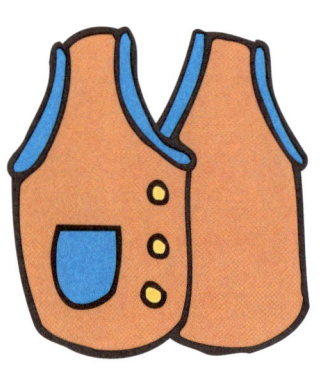

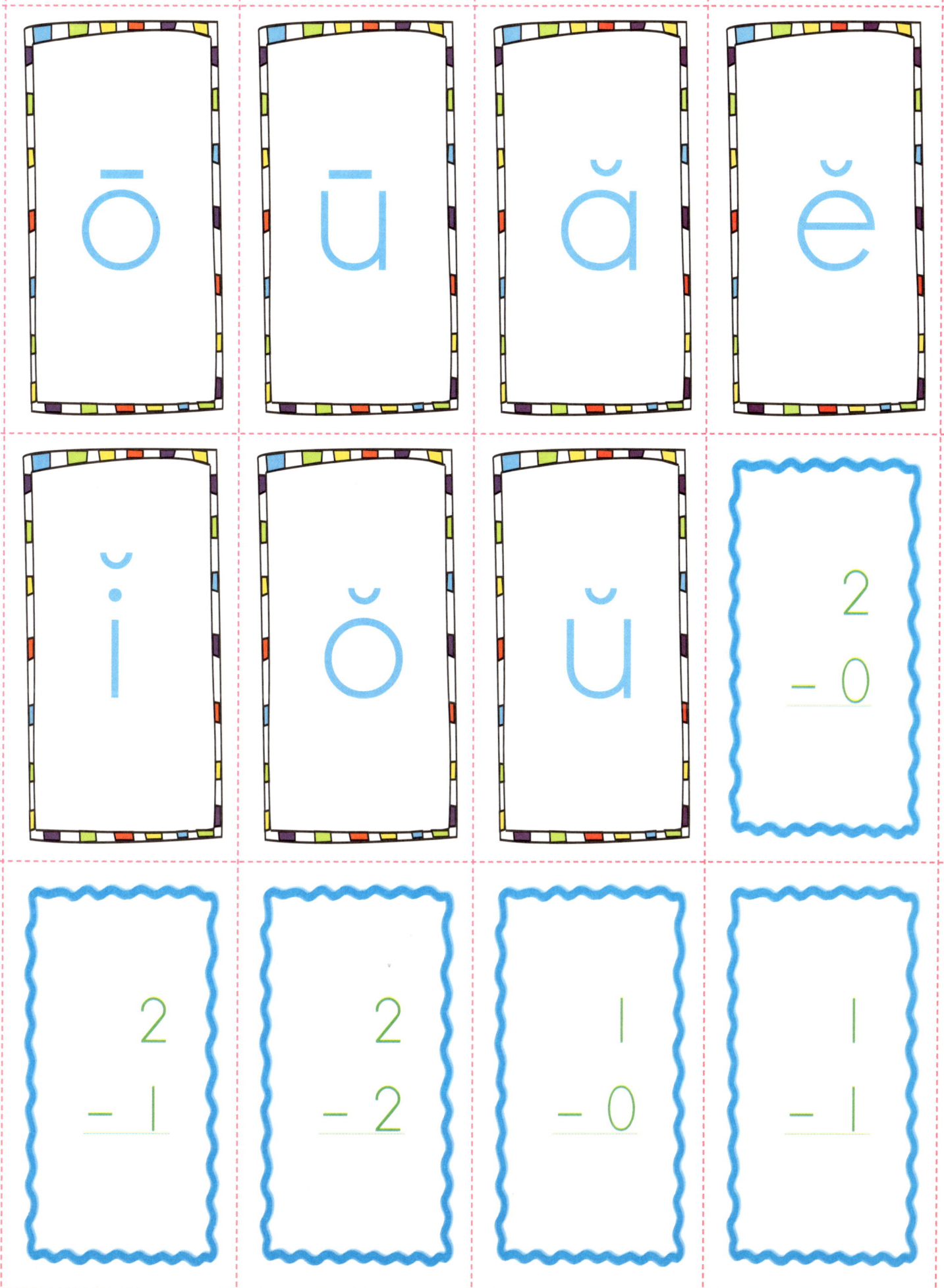

# Congratulations!

**you**

*Your Name*

have completed

**Summer Bridge Activities™** *for Young Christians*

_Ms. Hansen_
Miss Hansen's Signature

_M. Fredrickson_
Mr. Fredrickson's Signature

_____
Parent's Signature

*God is love.*
*God is love.*